JAMESTOWN

An American Legacy

❖

MARTHA W. MCCARTNEY

ACKNOWLEDGEMENTS

Any research project is a collaborative effort that involves specialists from numerous fields. Their contributions, individually and collectively, have made possible the production of this manuscript. In particular, I would like to thank James Haskett, David Riggs, Jane Sundberg, and Diane Stallings of the National Park Service; Cary Carson, Audrey Horning, Greg Brown, Heather Harvey and Andy Edwards of the Colonial Williamsburg Foundation; Tom Davidson of the Jamestown-Yorktown Foundation; and Dan Hawks, whose comments and encouragement were invaluable.

This publication was funded by Eastern National, a cooperating association of the National Park Service that supports research, education, and interpretive programs at Colonial National Historical Park.

Eastern National
Serving America's National Parks
and Other Public Trusts

Cover: *Jamestown Lifescape, mid-17th Century* by Keith Rocco

Table of Contents

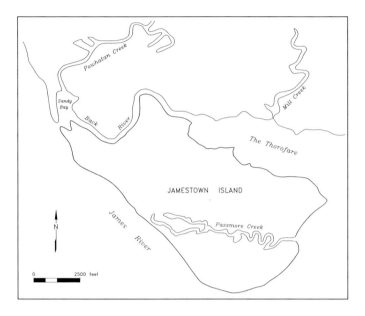

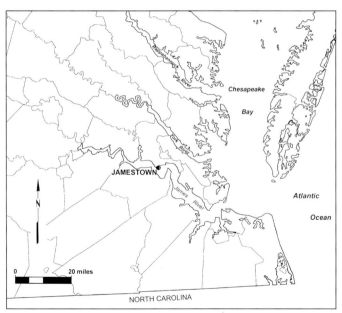

PROLOGUE

On May 13, 1607, the first permanent English settlement in North America was established in Virginia, at Jamestown. From the beginning, the fledgling colony's future was uncertain, for the settlers struggled to adapt to an unfamiliar environment. Nearly four hundred years later, Americans look to Jamestown as the birthplace of their great nation. Jamestown itself is an American legacy.

Some of Jamestown's legacies are a source of pain rather than pride. In 1619, newly arrived Africans were forced into a system of labor that eventually culminated in institutional slavery. They tended tobacco, the economic salvation of the colony, but they also contributed their knowledge and specialized skills. Like the Africans, Virginia Indians suffered mistreatment. Europeans' mistaken sense of superiority resulted in the displacement of these native people from their land.

Despite the tragedies, Jamestown remains a source of universal inspiration. Here, diverse cultures from three continents met and sometimes clashed. In time, a new way of life emerged, one that was based upon survival, experimentation, and adaptation. Among Jamestown's most significant legacies is the development of representative government and a legal code based upon English precedents.

As the story of Jamestown unfolds in the following pages, the lives of those who drew their sustenance from Virginia's lush natural resources, labored in the fields, tended children, conducted the business of government, or suffered the pangs of birth and death, reflect some of the major events of American history. Jamestown tells today's generations that sacrifices often are important to achieving lasting success. Jamestown also reminds us that the present is better understood when viewed through the lens of the past.

T B   20

$\mathcal{C}hapter$ 1

❖

NATURAL BEGINNINGS

JAMESTOWN ISLAND'S FIRST INHABITANTS

Thousands of years before the first European colonists arrived, American Indians inhabited Virginia's coastal plain. Though largely unrecorded, their early history is at least partly revealed to us through archaeological excavations.

Their lives moved with the rhythms of nature. In summer, Virginia's coastal plain, including Jamestown, offered a satisfying variety of fish, shellfish, and game. Cleared fields blossomed into planted gardens that often produced more food than could be eaten in one season. In winter, after the harvest, when cold weather made fishing an unpleasant and mostly unproductive endeavor, the natives moved inland in search of more plentiful game.

Villages, sustained by surplus food, gradually replaced the base camps common during earlier periods. Built on low-lying necks of land with rich, sandy soil, these villages usually were well organized. In some cases, a palisade of wooden posts ringed a cluster of relatively substantial houses. Village fields were never far away. Corn or maize, introduced into the region from Mexico, grew well in Virginia as did beans, squash, and tobacco. Women, children, and elderly men tilled the crops and cleared new fields using the slash-and-burn method. Archaeologists think that control of the food supply brought rank or

The broiling of their fish over the flame, an engraving by Theodore de Bry. Courtesy of the Jamestown -Yorktown Foundation.

status to certain individuals and led to the development of gradually more complex societies. The hundreds of villages that existed in Tidewater Virginia

The Towne of Secota, an engraving by Theodore de Bry. Courtesy of the Jamestown-Yorktown Foundation.

top: *A weroan or great Lorde of Virginia,* an engraving by Theodore de Bry. Courtesy of the Jamestown-Yorktown Foundation.

middle: *The manner of making their boates,* an engraving by Theodore de Bry. Courtesy of the Jamestown-Yorktown Foundation.

bottom: *Their manner of fishing in Virginia,* an engraving by Theodore de Bry. Courtesy of the Jamestown-Yorktown Foundation.

began to compete for territory and economic supremacy. Weaker tribes allied with stronger tribes for protection in times of war. Recovered objects, creatively and carefully made of stone, copper, and shell clearly reflect native beliefs and the importance of ceremonial life. The Algonquian language that they spoke distinguished them from other groups farther inland who communicated in Iroquoian, Sioux, and other tongues.

In 1607, when the first English colonists arrived in Virginia, a paramount chief named Wahunsunacock or Powhatan ruled much of the coastal plain's native population. A monarch in every sense of the word, he commanded the allegiance of many lesser kings (or werowances) and reigned over 32 districts with 150 villages of various sizes. According to contemporary descriptions Powhatan stood tall. Despite his age, probably in his 60s, he appeared strong and hardy. His well-proportioned body was topped with a head of gray hair. He retained an uncharacteristic beard, thin by European standards.

Captain John Smith, a habitual observer of life, wrote that Indian men spent most of their time hunting, fishing, and waging war. Women and children made mats, baskets, and pottery and raised the crops upon which their villages depended. Smith described the natives as generally tall and straight, with black hair and dusky complexions. Exceptionally strong and agile, they tolerated even the worst weather.

But European and native cultures differed in critical ways, differences destined to create misunderstanding and conflict. The natives considered land a part of the earth, like the sky, water and air, free for all to use and enjoy. They failed to comprehend the European concept of owning land. Status passed through native females while Europeans preferred a patriarchal model with fathers bequeathing wealth and status to their sons, usually the eldest. And, of course, the two cultures held vastly different views of religion. While the natives were open to the idea of a Christian deity, they saw little reason to renounce their own gods.

EUROPE'S INTEREST IN THE NEW WORLD

European interest in the natural wealth of the New World set the stage for increased contact with native peoples and the conflicts that resulted. Spain's formidable sea power and the 1494 Treaty of Tordesillas emboldened her leaders to claim virtually all of North America from the tip of Florida to the mouth of the St. Lawrence River. The English and French refused to be intimidated. Their continued interest in the New World made the Spanish understandably uneasy about the safety of their claims and the treasure fleets that returned with the bounty of the Western Hemisphere. Their concern was justified. In 1531 the Bristol merchant, Robert Thorne, urged England's King Henry VIII to seek a northern route to Asia. He led England's most vocal advocates of colonization by declaring, "No land uninhabitable nor sea unnavigable." In the imaginative and venturesome minds of some who studied maps of North America, the coastline south of the Chesapeake Bay became a potential haven for English privateers. Armed ships could hug the shoreline and then sail down and capture the heavy-laden Spanish treasure ships that rode the north-flowing Gulf Stream.

THE SPANISH JESUIT MISSION IN VIRGINIA

The Spanish near the peak of their global influence, took aggressive action to solidify their claims in the New World. In 1565 they established a military outpost at St. Augustine. Even earlier, a Spanish ship visiting the Chesapeake took aboard a native Indian boy, reputedly a chief's son, and transported him to Spain where he was converted to Christianity and renamed Don Luis. Later, the youth traveled to Cuba and St. Augustine, where Jesuit missionaries heard him speak of his native land, Ajacan. It was then that they resolved to sail north for the Chesapeake. Using Don Luis as an intermediary, they intended to spread their Christian message to other natives.

In 1570 a Spanish ship bearing eight Jesuit missionaries, Don Luis, and a Cuban boy named Alonzo de Olmos arrived in the Chesapeake Bay or Bahia de Santa Maria. They entered a broad, navigable river (the James) and continued inland to the converted native's homeland. They reached a creek, at the eastern end of Jamestown Island, and followed it inland. Then they portaged overland to another navigable stream (probably Queens Creek) which took them to the York River. Along the York the Jesuits began searching for a suitable place to establish a mission. Learning that there had been "six years of famine and death" and that many Indians had died or left in search of food, the missionaries sent word to St. Augustine that they needed corn for themselves and for the natives to plant in their gardens. The corn, they felt, would provide an opportunity to literally and figuratively sow the seeds of Christianity. But a few months later, when the relief ship arrived, canoes filled with Indian warriors attacked. A native captured in the melee revealed that the Jesuits were dead and only young Alonzo was alive.

Cuba's governor, Pedro Menendez de Aviles, refused to allow this attack on Spain's empire to stand unpunished. He decided to dispatch a small, armed vessel with a priest, thirty soldiers, and the Indian captured by the relief ship, to search for the Cuban boy and to learn the missionaries' fate. Retracing the Jesuits' route, they sailed up the James, entered College Creek, and continued inland a short distance before dropping anchor. When a group of natives came aboard to trade, the Spaniards noticed that one wore a piece of the missionaries' communion silver around his neck. They promptly seized their visitors and headed back downstream, fending off attacking warriors along the way. The Indians offered to return the Cuban boy, but when he failed to appear the Spaniards decided to leave and fired a departing shot into native onlookers. When they reached the mouth of the James, the Spanish discovered the boy and listened with dismay to his tale of fatal intrigue. As soon as Don Luis reached his homeland, the boy reported, he fled to his own people. The abandoned missionaries, left to fend for themselves, built a small hut. Responding to appeals for help, Don Luis feigned cooperation but ultimately he and his companions fell upon the Jesuits and killed them, sparing Alonzo on account of his youth.

Governor Menendez, frustrated in his attempt to capture Don Luis and disturbed by the apparently bloody demise of the missionaries, held an inquisition using the Cuban boy as translator. Although some of the Indians captured at College Creek were judged innocent and released, the remainder were baptized and hanged from the ship's yardarm. The Spaniards then weighed anchor leaving in their wake a legacy of dread and suspicion. The Jesuit mission site gradually faded into the forest.

ENGLAND CHALLENGES SPAIN'S CLAIM

Throughout the sixteenth century, English "sea dogs" became increasingly aggressive in challenging Spain's New World dominance. Martin Frobisher actively searched for a northwest passage to China, and Sir Francis Drake circled the world, boldly intruding into western lands that Spain and Portugal considered theirs. In June 1578 Sir Humphrey Gilbert obtained royal authority to seek any "remote heathen and barbarous lands" not already possessed by a Christian nation. After Gilbert's death, Queen Elizabeth I awarded his half-brother, Sir Walter Raleigh, a charter to all western lands between 33 and 40 degrees north.

Portrait of Sir Walter Raleigh. Courtesy of the Colonial Williamsburg Foundation.

Intrigued by those who fervently believed in the riches of the New World, Raleigh sent two ships on an exploratory voyage to America. By early July 1584 the mariners reached the Outer Banks inlet called "Hatarask" by the Indians. Taking in hand a twig and turf and affixing their monarch's seal to an upright post, they formally took possession of the region. With enthusiasm, they declared the soil "the most plentifull, sweete, fruitfull and wholsome of all the world." The woodlands appeared profuse and the Indians friendly.

Raleigh's claim was confirmed in December and, a month later, after receiving a knighthood, he was named lord and governor of Virginia. Immediately he began organizing an effort to establish a colony. Queen Elizabeth allowed him to name his new land Virginia in commemoration of her spinsterhood and furnished him with a ship and supplies. In all, seven ships bearing would-be colonists set sail in April 1585. But when the ships arrived in July, a cautious Roanoke Indian leader allowed only a hundred colonists to establish a settlement on Roanoke Island. The others were sent home.

By September 1585 Ralph Lane and his fellow adventurers had built a fort and some cottages. During the fall and winter months they ventured northward in a small boat and trekked overland to the mouth of the Chesapeake Bay. They explored the mainland west of Roanoke Island and chronicled their discoveries in reports and sketches intended for Raleigh. The exquisite drawings made by artist John White and the scientific writings of Thomas Harriot provide a remarkably detailed view of native life and the fauna and flora of the region's coastal plain. Ralph Lane noted that when summer came he intended to search for a better harbor within the territory that lay to the north. But by late May 1586, relations with the Indians had deteriorated. There were sporadic outbreaks of violence, and when Sir Francis Drake's fleet appeared on the Outer Banks in June, the Roanoke colonists, with little hesitation, abandoned their settlement and returned to England. There, Thomas Harriot's writings and John White's drawings and maps attracted widespread attention, prompting immediate plans for another colony. In May 1587 another 150 men, women, and children filed aboard ship and set sail, en route to Roanoke from Plymouth.

But these colonists faced trouble immediately. The Spanish Armada threatened English shipping. The expedition's Portuguese pilot landed the colonists on Roanoke Island, but then abandoned them. Within a month, John White, the fledgling settlement's governor, agreed to return to England for additional supplies. The colonists, at the time of his departure, were planning to move 50 miles inland. When they left, they agreed to carve their destination on a tree or post, using a cross-mark (+) if they were in distress. Although White reached England safely, his relief plan fell apart; no supplies reached the Roanoke colony.

It was mid-August of 1590 when John White once again went ashore on Roanoke Island. There he found traces of the colonists' settlement, but their belongings were gone. According to plan, they left word of their destination. A large post was inscribed "CROATAN," the Indians' name for Ocracoke Island, but the carved message included no cross-mark. Forced to return home without making contact, White never found the "Lost Colonists." They vanished into the wilderness, leaving future generations to ponder their fate. Meanwhile, Sir Walter Raleigh's personal fortunes took a dramatic turn for the worse. Disliked by King James I, Raleigh was found guilty of treason and imprisoned in the Tower of London. He lost his 1584 land claim and was eventually executed in 1618, ending attempts to establish a Roanoke colony.

VIRGINIA'S PROMISE

Although a 1604 peace treaty appeared to reduce tension between Spain and England, conflicts over western lands persisted. Spain's ambassador urged his superiors to destroy English colonies while they were small and vulnerable. He also tried to convince England's King James I that it was "much against good friendship and brotherliness" to populate Virginia.

But most English investors viewed colonization as a broadly based economic enterprise. Sir Thomas Smith, an investor in Raleigh's Roanoke ventures and the head of two important trading companies, ardently believed that Virginia held great economic potential and eventually supported the colony at Jamestown. Merchants in Bristol, Plymouth, and Exeter, involved in the profitable Newfoundland trade, also recognized Virginia's potential for profit. In 1605 sea captain George Weymouth visited North Virginia (New England) and noted

Portrait of Sir Thomas Smith. Courtesy of the Colonial Williamsburg Foundation.

its abundant natural resources, returning with more American Indian captives, who predictably piqued interest in the region.

Thus encouraged, King James I decided to pursue England's interest in North America, as long as peace with Spain could be preserved. On April 6, 1606, he issued a charter to the Virginia Company, a joint stock corporation headed by royal appointees. Company officials were to define the structure of

government within the region to be colonized and establish its legal framework. Two sub-units were created to administer approximately 1,500 miles of shoreline and adjacent lands. The Virginia Company of Plymouth was allocated New England, and the Virginia Company of London was assigned territory between 34 and 41 degrees north. As the London-based group's land lay at a more temperate latitude, its officials hoped to reap large profits from exporting hides, medicinal substances, timber products, minerals, and precious metals. They also hoped to make full use of the region's unlimited natural resources by manufacturing saleable products such as glass, iron, potash, pitch, and tar.

The Virginia Company Coat of Arms. Courtesy of the Colonial Williamsburg Foundation.

In 1607 the Virginia Company of Plymouth attempted to plant a colony at Sagadehoc in present day Maine. But the garrison, Fort Saint George, faltered and ultimately failed. Thus, through a twist of fate, the Virginia Company of London's settlement on the James River became America's first permanent English colony.

◆

Portrait of King James I. Courtesy of the Colonial Williamsburg Foundation.

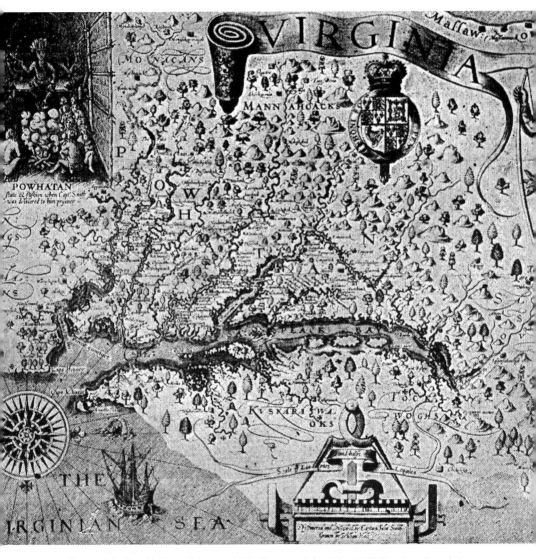

Captain John Smith's Map of Virginia, 1612. Courtesy of the Colonial Williamsburg Foundation.

Chapter 2

OUTPOST IN THE WILDERNESS

THE FIRST COLONISTS

On Saturday, December 20, 1606, three small ships caught the outbound tide and set sail from London. The *Susan Constant, Discovery,* and *Godspeed* moved slowly down the Thames, then anchored in the Downs, awaiting favorable winds. Finally, they headed out to sea on an adventure that changed the course of history.

To command this tiny fleet, Virginia Company officials chose Captain Christopher Newport, a sailor with unrivaled experience in navigating the American coastline. Captain John Smith, an experienced explorer and soldier-of-fortune with proven survival skills, and apparently others in the group had read the accounts of the Roanoke Island colony. Bartholomew Gosnold and Gabriel Archer, both veterans of previous New World voyages, were familiar with the natives. Along with Newport and Smith, they possessed a basic knowledge of the Algonquian language. Each faced the rigors of the Atlantic voyage and the challenges of colonial life without illusion. Their experience matched the role that a new colony inevitably would play as a military outpost of empire. But nearly half of Virginia's first settlers were gentlemen, scholars, artisans, and tradesmen, not laborers or sturdy yeoman farmers whose basic skills and physical conditioning might prove invaluable in a wilderness environment.

According to historian Phillip L. Barbour, the diverse members of the expedition were "Bound together by kinship, partnership and previous business experience" that included privateering.

The ships sailed south along the coasts of Spain and Portugal and then toward the Canary Islands. There they caught the Canary Current, which carried them

Captain Christopher Newport

In 1606, the Council of Virginia gave Captain Christopher Newport "sole charge and command" of all the persons aboard the three ships that set sail from England in December 1606 for North America. A seasoned mariner, Newport made several voyages to the West Indies before accepting command of the Jamestown venture. He would make five voyages to Virginia between 1606 and 1612.

In 1612, the East India Company employed Newport for a voyage to Persia. A contemporary remarked that Newport was "much commended . . . for his good services, delivering his charges, safely, discovering unknown places . . .." In 1614, the East India Company awarded him the title of Admiral and sent him on a second voyage to the East Indies.

In 1617, Newport docked at Java during yet another trip for the East India Company, died, and was buried at sea.

west across the Atlantic Ocean. In March 1607 they reached the West Indies where they paused for three weeks. Sailing north into the Gulf Current, Newport's fleet was swept toward Virginia.

After a difficult 18-week crossing, the three ships and 104 men and boys arrived safely on April 26, 1607. At Cape Henry, overlooking the Chesapeake, they erected a cross. Naturally apprehensive about their risky undertaking, subjected to cramped quarters, seasickness, boredom, and inferior food, some probably questioned the wisdom of their decision to leave England. Surely they speculated about who Virginia Company officials had chosen as the new colony's leaders. As soon as Captain Newport reached Virginia he opened a sealed box that contained the names of the seven men selected for the colony's first council. As the highest-ranking local officials, they held the authority to elect their own president. Transported inside this box, contained in these instructions, the rudiments of English common law landed in the New World.

During the colonists' first few days in Virginia, they sailed inland to explore the countryside. From time to time they ventured cautiously ashore. They found magnificent timber, fields covered with brilliantly colored flowers, lush vegetation, fertile soil, and an abundance of wildfowl, game, and seafood. Colonist George Percy declared Virginia a veritable paradise on earth. He saw

The Arrival of Settlers at Jamestown. Courtesy of the Mariners' Museum, Newport News, Virginia.

beech, oak, cedar, cypress, walnut, and sassafras trees, as well as strawberries, raspberries, mulberries, and some fruit and berries that he could not name. And amidst the wilderness he found large meadows that would make excellent pasture for cattle.

As the colonists moved up the broad river called the Powhatan, later the James, they encountered natives with ornamented bodies. They wore feathers in their hair and animal horns on their heads. Dressed in brightly colored furs, they were adorned with jewelry of bone, shell, and copper. According to John Smith, some of the Indians welcomed the newcomers hospitably, offering food and entertainment. Others, however, discharged arrows and then retreated from the colonists' retaliatory gunfire.

On May 12 Newport's fleet arrived at a promontory that the men named Archer's Hope. There the soil was fertile. Game was abundant. The timber stood tall and straight. In many ways Archer's Hope seemed an ideal site for a settlement, except for the shallow water that prevented ships from anchoring near the shore. For two weeks the colonists scouted along the river. Upstream from Archer's Hope they found a marsh-rimmed peninsula that resembled an island. There, where the river's channel ran so close to land that the colonists could moor their ships to trees, they established an outpost called James Fort or Jamestown, the first permanent English settlement in North America.

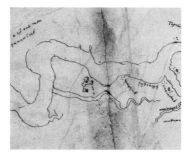

Map of Virginia, 1608. Ministerio de Educación, Cultura y Deporte. Archivo General de Simancas. MPD. IV-66.

Edged Weapons from the Jamestown Museum Collection. Courtesy of the National Park Service, Colonial National Historical Park.

Colonists Landing at Jamestown. Painting by Sidney King. Courtesy of the National Park Service, Colonial National Historical Park.

GETTING SETTLED

These first colonists, keenly aware of their vulnerability, built a primitive half-moon fort from the boughs of trees. Spain also claimed these lands, and all around lived the Pasbehay Indians, whose territory extended along the upper bank of the James River, between that of the Kecoughtans (near the mouth of the James) and the Weyanokes (above the Chickahominy River). During the colonists' first night on Jamestown Island, sentinels sounded an alarm around midnight when they spied Indians approaching in canoes.

After an Indian attack on May 26, Edward Maria Wingfield, the colony's elected president, agreed that a more substantial stronghold, palisaded and with mounted ordnance, should be built. One early writer described this second fort as triangular with a bulwark at each corner containing four or five pieces of ordnance. John Smith later claimed that continual threats from Indians around the periphery of the settlement motivated work on the new fort.

A week after the settlers completed their fort, Captain Newport set sail for England, and the realities of life on the edge of wilderness soon tested the courage of even the bravest colonist. Hunger became a way of life. Instead of digging a well for drinking water, they turned to the river described as a salty brew at high tide or a blend of slim and filth at low. Mosquitoes, ticks, flies, and countless other insects offered continual torment. Diseases like typhoid and dysentery began claiming lives. Sickness was so common that few colonists could walk or even stand. The men reportedly "were destroyed with cruel diseases as swellings, fluxes, [and] burning fevers," but "for the most part they died of famine." A small ladle of barley ground into meal and made into porridge equaled a daily ration of food. Although the Indians became bolder as they noted the settlers' flagging strength, they saw the colonists as potential allies and a source of interesting trade goods, and shared food that saved the colonists' lives.

Captain John Smith

Born in 1579 in Willoughby, England, John Smith left home as a teenager after his father died. He became a soldier of fortune, fighting in the Low Countries for Dutch independence against the Spanish, then traveling throughout the Mediterranean, eventually being captured by the Turks in Hungary. After escaping from slavery in Istanbul, he returned to England in the winter of 1604-05.

His adventures to exotic places continued when he became involved with the Virginia Company's plans to establish a permanent English colony in North America for profit. Smith would play an important role in providing the necessary leadership to ensure the survival of Jamestown.

During his brief tenure from May 1607 to the fall of 1609, Smith successfully traded for food with the Indians, explored the Chesapeake Bay, and restored order to dissenting fellow settlers. Eventually he was elected president of the colony in the fall of 1608. He instituted a policy of rigid discipline, strengthened defenses and encouraged farming with this admonishment, "He who does not work, will not eat." Unfortunately Smith was accidentally injured by burning gunpowder and returned to England for treatment, never to return to Virginia.

Based on Smith's writings of early Virginia, a wonderful account of the trials and tribulations of the first English settlers in establishing Jamestown and their encounters with the Virginia Indians survive. He died in England in 1631 at the age of 51.

THE PORTRAICTUER OF CAPTAYNE IOHN SMITH ADMIRALL OF NEW ENGLAND.

These are the Lines that shew thy Face; but those
That shew thy Grace and Glory, brighter bee:
Thy Faire-Discoueries and Fowle-Overthrowes
Of Salvages, much Civilliz'd by thee
Best shew thy Spirit; and to it Glory Wyn;
So, thou art Brasse without, but Golde within.

Portrait of Captain John Smith by Simon de Passe, 1616. Courtesy of the Library of Virginia, Richmond, Virginia.

THREE SUPPLIES OF NEW SETTLERS

Eight or nine months after Christopher Newport's departure, he returned to Virginia with 120 new immigrants. Weakened and hungry from the voyage, they discovered that neither food nor shelter awaited them. Thirty-eight of the original settlers survived, only ten were physically able to work. With clearly scrambled priorities, Newport, a Virginia Company officer, set the newcomers to work felling trees and making ship masts and clapboard that could be sold in England. He also sent them digging for gold ore, placing greater emphasis on making money for the Virginia Company than on assuring the colony's survival. Later, John Smith declared that during this very early period "our drinke was water, our lodgings, castles in the air." Smith's words echo those of Thomas Harriot, who declared that some of the Roanoke colonists languished for lack of English cities, "faire houses," or "daintie food." Evidently the lessons of the "Lost Colony" remained unlearned. "Many," wrote another eye-witness, "famished in holes in the ground," a reference to the rude shelters or pit-houses settlers fashioned by digging a cavity six or seven feet into the earth, lining it with bark or timbers, and then covering it with spars and bark or sod. Some built arbor-like cabins like those of the natives. They set closely spaced timber poles into the ground, bent them into arches and then covered them with bark.

Just after Newport's return, in early January 1608, a devastating, accidentally set fire swept through James Fort. It destroyed the colonists' dwellings, provisions, and much of the fort. Fortunately, Captain Newport remained on hand, and his mariners helped the colonists repair their homes and fortifications. Perhaps it was at this time that a rectangular, walled enclosure was built onto one side of the fort to accommodate what probably became the colonists' main living area. Captain Newport left Virginia on April 10, 1608, and ten days later Captain Francis Nelson straggled in with forty more settlers. Also unused to manual labor, they did assist in clearing about four acres of ground and building "a few poore houses."

About nine months later, seventy new immigrants, the Second Supply, landed at Jamestown. Among them were Mrs. Thomas Forest and her maid, Anne Burras, who married laborer John Laydon in late 1608. Their union, Virginia's first wedding, marked the beginning of family life in the colony. The Second Supply of new colonists also included 28 gentlemen, 14 tradesmen, and eight Germans and Poles, who had come to make pitch, tar, and potashes or lye. The addition of so many more mouths to feed exhausted the colony's food supply forcing the settlers to depend on the Indians for corn once again.

During this time, John Smith's experience as an explorer, coupled with his ability to cope with primitive living conditions, propelled him into a leadership role. Chosen president in September 1608, he tried to force the settlers to work toward their own support. Unsuccessful, he eventually dispersed the hungry colonists relieving cramped conditions within Jamestown. With characteristic self-confidence, he later marveled at all he had accomplished during his yearlong presidency. With only one carpenter, two blacksmiths, two sailors, a few laborers, Germans and Poles, and some "gentlemen, Tradesmen, Serving-men, libertines and such like," the colonists converted Jamestown's fort into a five-sided form that was strongly impaled with a 14 to 15 foot palisade. A church, storehouse, 40 or 50 houses, and "a faire well of fresh water" occupied the interior of the enclosure. Smith also said that the settlers built a blockhouse at the entrance to the island, experimented with glass making, and planted 100 acres of corn.

In May 1609 the Virginia Company received its second charter. Company officials now could choose a governor to serve as the colony's principal leader. The governor, in turn, could select the members of his Council, who served as his advisors. Given "full and absolute power and authority to correct, punish, pardon, governe and rule," this governor was not to be taken lightly. When Sir Thomas West (Lord De La Warr) was unable to assume his post as governor and captain-general of Virginia, Sir Thomas Gates, as lieutenant-governor, set sail with 500 new settlers (the Third Supply).

But Gates' fleet of nine ships got caught in a hurricane that blew them off course. One small catch perished at sea. The flagship, *Sea Venture*, which carried Gates, Sir George Somers, John Rolfe, and other notables, ran aground on the rocks of the Bermudas. By mid-August 1609, however, the seven sur-

Captain John Smith trading with the Powhatan Indians. Painting by Sidney King. Courtesy of the National Park Service, Colonial National Historical Park.

Portrait of Thomas West, Lord De la Warr. Courtesy of the Jamestown-Yorktown Foundation.

viving vessels limped into Jamestown, with more than 400 new colonists, including women and children. In just three days, the famished newcomers devoured a field of corn, the colony's main food supply. John Smith declared a large number of men in the Third Supply to be gallants hurried off to the colony to "escape evil destinies." When they found none of the luxuries to which they were accustomed, these "reckless young fops" declared Virginia "a miserie, a ruine, a death, a hell."

THE INFAMOUS STARVING TIME

The stage was now set for the desperate winter of 1609-1610, traditionally known as "The Starving Time." Still in command, Smith dispersed the colonists to new settlements at Nansemond, on the south side of the James River's mouth, and to the falls of the James on the north. After returning from an inspection tour, Smith was accidentally burned in a gunpowder explosion, forcing him to resign as president and in October to seek medical treatment in England. He never returned to Virginia again. In the absence of Smith's leadership, George Percy was persuaded to accept the position of president and was in command during this terrible winter. Faced with retaliatory attacks by the Powhatans, sickness, disease, and malnutrition, the situation deteriorated rapidly.

Most of the colonists returned to Jamestown where extreme hunger forced them to live off roots dug from the frozen ground and whatever wild animals they could capture. They ate "those Hogges, Dogges, and horses that were then in the colony, together with rats, mice, snakes or what vermin or carrion soever we could light on . . . that would fill either mouth or belly." Some colonists fled to their mortal enemies, the Indians. Others claimed that cannibalism occurred. Smith, based on reports that he received from first-hand accounts, wrote that the colonists' could blame no one but themselves for nearly starving. They were so lazy, he contended that they failed to plant crops. This was also a time of a severe drought that would limited the food that could be grown.

The Starving Time forced the colony to the brink of extinction. By May 1610, when Sir Thomas Gates and a hundred or so of his shipmates finally reached Virginia in two vessels built of Bermuda cedar, he found the fort in ruins and the surviving colonists "famished and at the point of death." So pitiful was their plight that he decided to evacuate them to Newfoundland, where they could recuperate and return to England. In the second week of June the settlers loaded their belongings aboard Gates' ships and buried their cannon. Some wanted to set the fort ablaze, but Gates stopped them. Bidding farewell to Jamestown, they set out down the river. Only the timely arrival (June 1610) of Lord De La Warr's three ships bearing provisions and a supply of new settlers, averted abandonment of the colony. Although ill health forced Governor De La Warr to withdraw to the West Indies in March 1611, during his short tenure he set about strengthening and rebuilding the colony. He had new houses erected "in and about James Town," along with batteries for iron and steel. He sent Gates to England to procure supplies and even more colonists. William Strachey, who arrived in Virginia in May 1610 and left in April 1611, described Jamestown's fort with careful detail. The triangular palisade consisted of sturdy posts and planks set four feet into the ground. The wall facing the river stretched for 420 feet; the other two sides measured 300 feet each. A market place, storehouse, court de garde, and chapel occupied the interior.

The Arrival of Lord De la Warr. Painting by Sidney King. Courtesy of the National Park Service, Colonial National Historical Park.

MARTIAL LAW

In May 1611 Sir Thomas Dale, then second in command to Lord De La Warr, arrived in Virginia with a fleet bearing 300 new settlers and soldiers as well as provisions, supplies, livestock, and seeds to grow garden crops. A military man with extensive experience in the Netherlands, Dale found Jamestown's condition appalling. He concluded that the colony could be defended against neither Indians nor foreign foes. He evidently agreed with John Smith—the settlers wasted their energy quarreling among themselves rather than growing food and building shelter. Rightly or wrongly, Dale attributed the colony's woes to a lack of strong leadership. His solution was drastic. Within a month of his arrival he declared martial law. This harsh military code of justice included moral and religious rules and, as was common in the seventeenth century, frequently used the death penalty for even minor infractions of the law. When he left Virginia in 1616, the colony was on a relatively sound footing and its survival was assured. Two invaluable lessons had been learned. First, the settlers could and, in fact, had to grow their own food. Second, the colony's success depended upon the personal initiative of its inhabitants. For the first time in Virginia, as of 1614, private ownership of land was allowed.

Dale, in response to the Virginia Company's orders to build the colony's princi-

Pocahontas

Facts about the early life of Pocahontas are scant. She was a favorite daughter of Chief Powhatan, ruler of the Powhatan Indians in Virginia. Born around 1595, she was probably 12 when the English arrived at Jamestown in 1607. Pocahontas visited the fort with gifts of corn so desperately needed for survival by the English.

The legend of Pocahontas saving the life of Captain John Smith when he was brought before her father as a prisoner may never be proven as fact. Smith left for England in 1609. There is no mention of Pocahontas until the English took her prisoner in 1613 at a time when the relationship between the settlers and the Powhatans had turned hostile. While in captivity, she was baptized into the Christian faith, took the name Rebecca, and married an Englishman named John Rolfe in April 1614.

The marriage of Pocahontas and John Rolfe initiated a period of peace for many years. In 1615 she bore a son named Thomas. The following year the Rolfe family embarked on a journey to England as guests of the Virginia Company. While in England, Pocahontas was introduced to royalty and came in contact with her old friend Captain John Smith for a brief visit. In March 1617, while preparing to return home to Virginia, Pocahontas became ill and died unexpectedly at Gravesend where she was buried. John Rolfe returned to Virginia alone, leaving his young son in the care of family members. John Rolfe died in 1622, but his son Thomas later returned to Virginia to fulfill his parent's dreams for the future.

Pocahontas by Simon de Passe, 1616. Courtesy of Virginia Historical Society, Richmond, Virginia.

pal town in a healthier, more defensible location, established several new settlements toward the head of the James River. At Jamestown he had the colonists dig a new well and build a stable, houses for munitions and powder, a structure where sturgeon could be cured, a wharf, a barn, a forge, and a blockhouse overlooking the Back River. He put men to work making brick and planting crops and he sent some settlers to Virginia's Eastern Shore to render salt from seawater, so that fish could be preserved. Dale introduced several innovative policies designed to reward colonists who worked toward their own support. He also opened the colony to Dutch trade. He dealt with the Indians from a position of strength, and relations with them improved. Meanwhile, John Rolfe fell in love with Powhatan's

The Marriage of Pocahontas. Courtesy of the National Park Service, Colonial National Historical Park.

daughter, Pocahontas, who had been kidnapped in 1613, and married her on April 5, 1614. Their union led to several years of peace, years used by the colonists to strengthen their foothold in Virginia.

AGRICULTURE: THE KEY TO SUCCESS

Despite early dreams of discovering gold, farming actually held the key to Virginia's success. Jamestown Island had been thickly wooded when the colonists first arrived but, with backbreaking labor, fields had been cleared and fenced. In 1616, of the fifty people who lived on Jamestown Island, 32 farmed. And, during Dale's administration, John Rolfe developed a strain of sweet-scented tobacco that became very popular in England and revolutionized Virginia's economy. It quickly became such a valuable crop that settlers used it as currency. The promise of tobacco proved so seductive that local officials had to dictate civic responsibilities otherwise ignored. Tenant farmers, those who owned three acres of land, had to defend their own settlements and the colony, perform 31 days public service a year, provide their own households with food and clothing and contribute 2 1/2 barrels of Indian corn per male household member to the common store. No one could plant tobacco until he had put in two acres of corn per male household member. Once that basic obligation was fulfilled, these farmers could raise as much tobacco as they wished.

Under Dale's leadership, Jamestown appeared to have reordered the dangerous priorities of its earliest years. According to Ralph Hamor, the secretary of the

A tobacco plant as depicted by Nicolas Menardes 1577.

colony, Jamestown was "reduced into a handsome forme" with "two faire rowes of howses" each with two stories and an upper garret or corn loft. "Three large and substantiall store houses," at least when filled, provided insurance against possible crop failures. Well provisioned, the town also was now well defended. "Newly and strongly impaled," Jamestown had "a faire platforme for ordnance" in the west bulwark. Elsewhere on the island were "some very pleasant, and beautifull howses, two Blockhouses, to observe and watch lest the Indians at any time should swim over the back river and come into the island, and certain other farme howses." Gates' own garden reportedly had small apple and pear trees that had sprouted from seeds planted the previous year.

Groups of poorly provisioned immigrants continued to arrive sick and famished, sometimes introducing rampantly infectious diseases into the colony. But Company officials now accepted the fact that new immigrants needed food and shelter while they recovered from their ocean voyage and became acclimated to the environment. Every new arrival reportedly received a year's supply of corn and rent-free use of "a handsome howse of some foure roomes or more, if he have a family," plus "12 English acres of ground adjoining thereto, very strongly

Harvesting Tobacco. Painting by Sidney King. Courtesy of the National Park Service, Colonial National Historical Park.

impailed, which ground is allotted to him for rents, gardaine hearbs and corn." One of the guesthouses built to accommodate newcomers stood four miles west of Jamestown, near the mouth of the Chickahominy River.

When Dale left Virginia in May 1616, few of his policies survived. Within a year Jamestown reportedly again was in disarray. The "marketplace and streets and all other spare places [were] planted with tobacco." Although Virginia Company officials recognized that the colony critically needed farmers and laborers to produce a dependable and adequate food supply and women to establish homes, many colonists preferred to plant tobacco instead of food crops. Then they complained about hunger while awaiting supplies from England. The "hard way of living," one early writer explained was not a lifestyle to which gentlemen and urbanites could readily adapt, even willingly. Instead they bartered with Indians for food and sometimes took it by force, making enemies in the process. John Pory, in 1619, captured the mood of the colony. Virginia, he wrote, was ideal for agriculture and the colony's riches lay in tobacco. Even the cowkeeper at Jamestown apparently strutted about in flaming silk. The wife of a former London collier sported a silk suit and a fine beaver hat with a pearl buckle. Such conspicuous consumption, made possible by a boom in tobacco prices, threatened to cloud colonial judgment and obscure the practical lessons taught by empty bellies.

Sir George Yeardley

A trusted friend of Governor Sir Thomas Gates, Yeardley arrived in Virginia in 1610. Gates appointed him Captain of the Guard. He was later named acting governor of the colony. He returned to England and was designated Governor of Virginia and was knighted by King James I in 1618.

When Sir George arrived in Virginia in 1619, he implemented the Virginia Company's Great Charter that established a system of laws, representative government, and private land ownership. Consequently, the first legislative assembly in the English colonies met on July 30, 1619.

In August 1619, Sir George traded for Africans who had arrived on a Dutch vessel at present day Hampton Roads. These were probably the first people from Africa to arrive in Virginia.

Sir George encouraged the financial growth of the colony, recognizing the importance of tobacco as a cash crop. He encouraged economic diversity, such as ironworks, silk production, and the cultivation of flax and silkgrass, to strengthen the economic viability of the colony.

By 1622, Sir Francis Wyatt became the new governor, allowing Sir George to devote more time to his private concerns. Yeardly, his wife, Lady Temperance, and their three children lived in a modest house in the New Towne section of Jamestown with 24 servants, of which eight were African. He served as governor for a second time in 1626 and died the following year.

Meeting of the First Legislative Assembly, 1619. Painting by Sidney King. Courtesy of the Association for the Preservation of Virginia Antiquities.

THE VIRGINIA COMPANY'S GREAT CHARTER

In London, Company investors found the costs of developing and maintaining a colony overwhelming. A third charter, granted by King James I in 1612, provided little relief. They needed a new outlook, an entirely new approach to colonization. Prepared for innovation by necessity, in 1618 the Virginia Company ratified the so-called Great Charter. Although company officials would chose Virginia's governor and his Council of State, this charter granted colonists the right to elect burgesses via popular vote. These burgesses, white men with a personal investment in the colony, would meet periodically in a general assembly. A judicial system akin to local English law would replace the harsh, arbitrary administration of martial law. A land policy that allowed colonists to own real estate and to work for personal gain would recognize and encourage private initiative. The Great Charter, it seems, deserves its name. It not only planted seeds of free enterprise in American soil, it transplanted both English common law and representative government to Virginia.

THE BEGINNING OF REPRESENTATIVE GOVERNMENT

On April 17, 1619, Virginia's new governor, Sir George Yeardley, arrived in the colony to assume the reins of government. In accord with his instructions, the colony was subdivided into four corporations or boroughs, each vast in size spanning both sides of the James River. The eleven settlements within those corporations were invited to elect delegates or burgesses to convene in an assembly that would write the colony's laws.

On July 30, 1619, the members of America's first legislative assembly gathered in Jamestown's church. Present were Governor Yeardley, his six councilors and two burgesses from almost all of the colony's settlements. Captain William Powell and Ensign William Spence represented Jamestown Island's inhabitants, who were residents of the corporation of James City. The Reverend Richard Buck offered a prayer for guidance. Then, John Pory, the assembly's speaker, read aloud excerpts from the Great Charter and reviewed two of the four books of laws that had been sent to the colony. The burgesses formed two committees to study the remaining books of laws and to petition the King for any changes that they felt necessary. Before adjourning, they adopted laws against idleness, gambling, drunkenness, and "excesse in apparel," as well as against theft and murder. They decided to regulate trade with the American Indians and to limit the number allowed to live and work within the settlements. They required colonists to provide their households with a year's supply of corn (or maize), storing some for use in times of need, and to plant vineyards, mulberry trees, and silk flax. Tobacco growers had to follow certain procedures when preparing their crop for market. No one was allowed to venture farther than 20 miles from home, visit Indian towns, or undertake a voyage longer than seven days without obtaining permission from governing officials. Endorsing the close link between church and state, they required ministers to make note of all christenings, marriages, and burials and to report to the authorities anyone suspected of committing moral offenses such as intoxication, fornication, or swearing. Household heads had to furnish the secretary of the colony with a list of those under their care.

With laws now in place, the administration of justice became important. At Jamestown the governor and his Council convened regularly as a court. By 1625 there were local courts in two of the colony's corporations and one on the Eastern Shore.

LAND AND LABOR

One of the most important features of the Great Charter made private land ownership possible. This new policy, known as the headright system, enticed prospective immigrants to seek their fortune in Virginia. Under this system, those with ready cash benefited the most. Investors in Virginia Company stock were entitled to 100 acres per share. Ancient Planters (those who immigrated to Virginia at their own expense and lived there for at least three years prior to Sir Thomas Dale's 1616 departure) also received 100 acres of land. Both Virginia Company investors and the Ancient Planters became eligible for an additional hundred acres when their first land allotment was planted. Those who came later, paid the cost of their own passage, and stayed in the colony for three years, were entitled to 50 acres of land. Anyone who underwrote the cost of another's transportation to Virginia became eligible for 50 acres on his or her behalf. Thus, successful planters, by importing hired workers for their plantations, could fulfill their need for labor while amassing additional land. Many people owned two or more tracts and circulated among them. Groups of investors sometimes absorbed the cost of outfitting and transporting prospective colonists, on whose behalf they acquired land and established private or "particular" plantations. The opportunity to reap substantial profits from growing tobacco while accumulating land fueled the spread of settlement.

Tobacco Pipes from the Jamestown Museum Collection. Courtesy of the National Park Service, Colonial National Historical Park.

Virginia planters, after they first arrived, typically constructed crude huts before erecting weatherproof but still insubstantial frame houses. Building such a simple dwelling or "Virginia house" enabled patentees to legitimatize their land claims while fulfilling the need for basic shelter. Renting land to tenants and providing low cost shelter to servants also encouraged the proliferation of impermanent housing.

The headright system led to a hierarchy of labor as well. Indentured servants or a minor's guardian usually signed a contract with an agent, agreeing to exchange a certain number of years work for transportation to Virginia. The agent then sold the contract to a colonial planter. In the beginning, many of Virginia's indentured servants were respectable citizens from the English middle class. At first, young males, particularly those in their late teens or early 20s, outnumbered females six to one. But both men and women from a broad cross-section of society, including yeoman farmers, husbandmen, artisans, and laborers sailed to Virginia.

Those who acquired indentured servants had to provide them with food, clothing, and shelter and could exact labor under certain conditions, using what the law deemed reasonable discipline. Indentured servants who were field hands usually toiled from dawn to dusk, six days a week, during the growing season. Adults usually served for four years, whereas those under 15 sometimes were bound to seven or more years. Literate servants or those with special skills could negotiate for shorter terms. When a contract expired the servant received "freedom dues," usually a quantity of corn and clothing. Former servants often leased land until they could acquire some of their own. New immigrants did likewise while fulfilling the headright system's residency requirements.

PUBLIC LAND

In addition to private land ownership, the Great Charter also specified that special tracts of land would be used to produce income for Company investors and

A Variety of Artifacts from the 1930s Archeology Excavations. Courtesy of the National Park Service, Colonial National Historical Park.

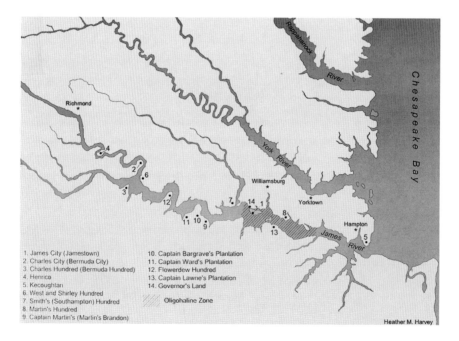

1. James City (Jamestown)
2. Charles City (Bermuda City)
3. Charles Hundred (Bermuda Hundred)
4. Henrico
5. Kecoughtan
6. West and Shirley Hundred
7. Smith's (Southampton) Hundred
8. Martin's Hundred
9. Captain Martin's (Martin's Brandon)
10. Captain Bargrave's Plantation
11. Captain Ward's Plantation
12. Flowerdew Hundred
13. Captain Lawne's Plantation
14. Governor's Land

▨ Oligohaline Zone

Heather M. Harvey

Early Settlements along the James River. Drawing by Heather M. Harvey, based upon information from the author. Courtesy of the Colonial Williamsburg Foundation.

to support high-ranking officials and clergy. By 1620 each of the four boroughs laid out 3,000 acres for Company lands. A 3,000-acre tract called the Governor's Land lay just west of Jamestown Island. The incumbent governor could lease this land to tenants or place his own servants there to work on his behalf. Immediately upstream was an equally large tract known as the Company Land. The Virginia Company intended to place its own indentured servants and tenants there to earn profits for investors. Land assigned to the corporation of James City's minister lay just east of Jamestown Island. The clergy, like other public officials, could occupy or rent their land allotments.

VIRGINIA'S FIRST BLACK IMMIGRANTS

But this was not an era of universal progress for individual rights and free enterprise. In August 1619, when a Dutch frigate, fresh from a plundering expedition in the West Indies, sailed into Hampton Roads, Virginia stood at another crossroad. At Old Point Comfort the vessel's captain struck a deal with Governor George Yeardley and merchant Abraham Peirsey. He agreed to exchange 20-some of the black captives that he held aboard his ship for provisions. Loaded onto another ship, these captives were brought to Jamestown where they were placed into servitude. Soon after the Dutch frigate's departure, a ship called the Treasurer left one or more Africans in Virginia. Although the concept of institutionalized slavery did not arise until much later, distinctive appearance, unfamiliar language, and cultural background set these involuntary immigrants apart from the other colonists and placed them at a decided disadvantage. Their Jamestown experience formed yet another chapter in a bewildering and anguishing journey. Captured in their African homeland, they were tied together and marched overland to the coast. There, they were sold again to traders, imprisoned, and branded. Loaded aboard overcrowded ships destined for North and South America, many died.

JAMESTOWN ISLAND DURING THE 1620S

As Jamestown entered the 1620s, it already was a fledgling urban community. By March 1620 there were 892 European colonists living in Virginia, with males outnumbering females by nearly seven to one. There were 32 blacks (17 women and 15 men) and four Indians who, like the blacks, were "in ye service of severall planters," some probably in the Jamestown households of Sir George Yeardley and Captain William Peirce. The Virginia colonists had a relatively ample supply of livestock and military equipment. There were more than 220 "habitable houses," not counting barns and storehouses. A year or so later, with 117 people, Jamestown Island ranked as the colony's most populous settlement.

Civic activities associated with church and state probably took place near the site of the old fort, where the marketplace, a pillory, and a whipping post were

Arrival of African Americans to Jamestown 1619. Painting by Sidney King. Courtesy of Colonial Williamsburg Foundation.

Arrival of the Young Women at Jamestown, 1621. Courtesy National Park Service, Colonial National Historical Park.

located. Meanwhile, residential development concentrated in New Towne, to the west of Orchard Run, where sometime prior to 1624 lots and streets were laid out along the water front. Many of the patents for New Towne lots cited earlier legislation enacted "to encourage building." Several lots abutted a road that skirted the riverbank. Back Street, and its developed lots, formed the back line of this first tier of lots.

Most of those who owned New Towne lots were wealthy merchants, prominent public officials, or both. It was here that Sir John Harvey, Ralph Hamor,

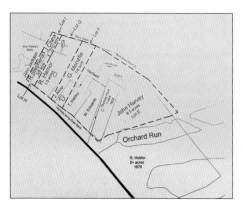

and fort captain William Peirce built houses. Peirce's new dwelling served as the collection point for the tobacco levied as taxes. Peirce's wife, Joan, "an honest and industrious woman" who had lived in the colony for many years, reportedly had "a garden at Jamestown containing 3 or 4 acres" from which she harvested nearly 100 bushels of excellent figs in a year. The Peirces' daughter, Jane, married John Rolfe after the death of Pocahontas in 1617.

Layout of early waterfront lots in the New Towne.
Map by Christina A. Kiddle and Heather M. Harvey.
Courtesy of the Colonial Williamsburg Foundation.

A policy requiring all incoming ships to pause at Jamestown before going elsewhere brought a steady stream of commerce to the island and profits to local businessmen. George Menefie, the official merchant of the corporation of James City from 1620 until at least 1637, owned a waterfront lot in the New Towne. Several other prominent merchants (Richard Stephens, John Chew, William Perry, John Pountis, and Edward Blaney) owned and occupied New Towne lots during the 1620s.

At the periphery of New Towne were somewhat larger parcels that belonged to Sir Francis Wyatt, Dr. John Pott, Sir George Yeardley, Secretary Richard Kemp, Sir John Harvey, and Captain Roger Smith. An 80-acre farm owned by Ancient Planter Richard Kingsmill abutted Back Creek and bordered east and south upon what became known as Kingsmill Creek.

In the eastern end of Jamestown Island were a dozen or more 12 acre plots laid out sometime prior to 1624. Ancient Planters owned almost all of them. This suggests that the eastern end of the island was purposefully carved up into small farmsteads at a very early date, perhaps between 1611 and 1616 under Sir Thomas Dale, who had his own 12 acre plot in the vicinity of Goose Hill. According to John Rolfe, some of the colony's Ancient Planters were the first to develop their own land. Ensign William

A Jamestown Home. Painting by Sidney King. Courtesy of the National Park Service, Colonial National Historical Park.

Spence, for example, came to Virginia in 1608 and settled on a 12 acre tract at the extreme eastern end of Jamestown Island. This clustering of Ancient Planters' farmsteads in the eastern end of Jamestown Island indicates that homes, in fact, were scattered throughout the island, a pattern confirmed by recent archaeological digs.

The homes of tradesmen and artisans also were scattered about Jamestown Island. During the mid-1620s, George Clarke, John Jackson, and John Jefferson were actively employed as gunsmiths. Jackson owned a New Towne lot on the waterfront next door to two merchants. Blacksmith William Briscoe's land was at the mouth of Orchard Run. Merchant George Menefie lived in New Towne but owned a forge at the western end of the island, near the old fort site. Thomas Passmore, a carpenter, and John Norton, a smith, had 12-acre parcels in the east-central portion of the island, as did feathermaker John Radish (Reddish) and joiner Thomas Grubb. During the mid-1620s shipbuilder Thomas Nunn and his men, sent to Virginia by the Company of Shipwrights, lived on Jamestown Island.

Sometime prior to 1624, at Glasshouse Point, the Italian glassworkers Vincencio, Bernardo, and three others attempted a second "tryall of glass." By 1625 they had withdrawn across the river to George Sandys' plantation and were clamoring to return home. Archaeological evidence near the banks of the

The 1622 Indian Uprising, an engraving by Theodore de Bry. Courtesy of the National Park Service, Colonial National Historical Park.

James River and Pitch and Tar Swamp confirms the presence of potters, apothecaries, brewers, bakers, and other specialized workers on Jamestown Island.

THE 1622 INDIAN UPRISING

The promise of prosperity that accompanied the first years of the 1620s did not last. Following the death of Pocahontas in 1617 and her father, Chief Powhatan, in 1618, local native leaders, particularly the charismatic paramount chief, Opechancanough, adopted a more militant attitude toward the Jamestown colonists. Perhaps threatened by the apparent success of the colony, the warriors of the Powhatan Chiefdom, on Friday, March 22, 1622, launched a carefully orchestrated attack upon the sparsely inhabited plantations along the James River. In a desperate attempt to drive the colonists from their soil, the natives killed nearly 350 men, women, and children in one day, somewhat more than a third of Virginia's settlers. Contemporary accounts reveal that the Indians entered the homes of the unsuspecting colonists as guests and then fell upon them, sometimes mutilating their corpses. At Archer's Hope, just east of

Jamestown Island, several people were killed although no lives were lost at Jamestown itself, where the settlers received word of the impending attack.

In the wake of the uprising, the Indians returned to several outlying plantations, forced their inhabitants to leave, and put their homesteads to the torch. The governor, Sir Francis Wyatt, declared martial law and ordered the colonists to withdraw to Jamestown or one of several other fortified settlements. At Jamestown the influx of refugees created severe food shortages and hastened the spread of contagious diseases, especially during the summer months. When new immigrants arrived, the death rate soared. Meanwhile, the colonists staged retaliatory raids on Indian villages, burning their houses and cutting down their corn. Virginia Company officials, though sympathetic to the settlers' plight, blamed them for settling so far apart that they could not easily unite for defense. Conversely, they insisted that it was a matter "of absolute necessitie" that the colonists reoccupy their plantations.

In early April 1623 Opechancanough sent word that "blud enough had already been shedd on both sides" and that his people were starving because the colonists were destroying their food supply. He offered to return some English captives and to allow the colonists to plant in peace, if his people could do the same. Although distrustful, the governor and Council agreed to a truce. The Indians, meanwhile, exchanged 19 female prisoners for some glass beads. Dr. John Pott of Jamestown, who redeemed one of the women with two parcels of beads, detained her as a servant in his home. Later, she claimed that working for him was little different than "her slavery with the Indians." Captain William Tucker, a veteran of the Dale years, gained notoriety by attempting to kill Opechancanough and other Indian leaders with poisonous wine raised in toast to a spurious peace treaty.

A few months later, the colonists began returning to their plantations. In the end, it was probably the common knowledge that abandoned Virginia land quickly grows up in underbrush that impelled the planters to return so quickly to their homesteads. Many were now armed with outmoded military equipment Virginia Company officials obtained from the Tower of London. One man claimed that planters were obliged to work "with our Hoe in one hand, and our peece [gun] or sword in the other." Occasional retaliatory raids kept the Indians at bay. The colonists were ordered to enclose their dwellings with palisades and were forbidden to trade with the Indians. Plans to build a palisade across the James-York peninsula languished without action for another decade. Colonial officials declared March 22, 1622, a holy day to be commemorated with prayer and fasting.

THE VIRGINIA COMPANY'S DEMISE

The Indian raids devastated the colony. During the winter of 1622-1623 Bermuda's ex-governor, Captain Nathaniel Butler, visited Virginia. He dispatched a scathing account to England, claiming that new immigrants could be seen "dyinge under hedges and in the woods" where their corpses lay unburied for days. He said that the colony's ironworks were destroyed, and its "Furnaces for Glass and Pots" were at a standstill. He added that Jamestown was unfortified and had only three pieces of ordnance for defense. Other critics alleged that Jamestown's wharf was in ruins and that the tide regularly inundated goods put ashore. One man even asserted that the colonists now longed for a return to martial law. But those who had endured the rigors of Sir Thomas Dale's government insisted that his policies had yielded immense pain without substantive gain. Ultimately, politics and insuperable financial problems took their toll, and in 1624 the Virginia Company's third and final charter was revoked. Although there were attempts to reinstitute company ownership, most colonists believed they would fare better under the Crown. By 1626 some of the Virginia Company's land had come into private hands and its indentured servants had been set free.

John Rolfe and Tobacco. Courtesy of the Jamestown-Yorktown Foundation.

LIFE IN THE COLONY

Demographic records compiled during 1624 and 1625 reveal that despite considerable hardships, family life had taken root in Virginia. Households often consisted of a married couple and one or more children, plus a small number of indentured servants. Many families included the children from prior marriages. Thus, stepsiblings, half-siblings, and full-blooded relatives tended to follow a parent or stepparent through a series of marriages often shortened by death. Orphans, widows, and invalids received care in the homes of those willing to take them in. The accumulation of wealth through successive marriages and the hardships that were a part of frontier life probably made widows and widowers eager to remarry. As the colony became better established, more women came to Virginia, and the number of marriages and births rose.

The February 1624 census reveals that 183 people then lived within Jamestown proper; 39 others resided elsewhere on the island. But an alarming 89 Jamestown Island inhabitants had died in less than a year. In January 1625,

Taking Slaves to Market. Courtesy of the Colonial Williamsburg Foundation.

when a new tabulation was made, the population had slipped even more; 175 people resided on Jamestown Island with two-thirds in Jamestown. Nine blacks (three men and six women) resided in urban Jamestown, which had 21 houses, three storehouses, a church, and a large court of guard. Elsewhere on the island were another ten houses. The colonists who resided upon Jamestown Island generally were better equipped and provisioned than those who lived elsewhere. They also had more livestock.

Despite serious setbacks, by the mid-1620s the Virginia colony was so firmly established that few doubted it would survive. The settlers had demonstrated that they could produce their own food supply. The headright system enticed would-be colonists to seek their fortunes in Virginia, whereas the opportunity to reap substantial profits from growing tobacco, a highly marketable commodity, served to fuel the spread of settlement. Despite native opposition, the colonists were in Virginia to stay.

❖

Tobacco Wharf Scene, Frye-Jefferson Cartouche. Courtesy of the Colonial Williamsburg Foundation.

Chapter 3

✦

THE COLONY MATURES

MAINTAINING LAW AND ORDER

As the population increased and communities developed, disagreements among neighbors sometimes ended up in court. Those who lived on privately-owned plantations sought justice from a local commander or leader. Others had to appear before the Governor's Council, which convened regularly as the Quarter Court. Cases ranged from offenses against religious laws, failing to pay church dues, or hunting hogs on Sunday, for example, to capital crimes such as murder and treason.

Many of the punishments handed down during the 1620s and 30s today would seem barbaric. A man's ears might be cut off for perjury or he might be whipped for a sex offense. But the seventeenth century was a brutal, bloody, and superstitious era in which corporal punishment—hanging, maiming, and dismemberment—was permissible under the law. Belief in witchcraft, omens, apparitions, and other supernatural phenomena was common. Virginia's first accused witch, Joan Wright, lived in the east end of Jamestown Island with her husband, Robert.

In a society that prized reputation and status, insults were serious. One Jamestown Island resident ran afoul of the law when he made disparaging remarks about a local minister. Another was summoned to court for calling a neighbor a "Virginia whore." Slanderers usually had to apologize publicly or post a bond guaranteeing good behavior.

When high ranking officials insulted one another, they usually knelt in church and took communion together, signifying their willingness to put the matter behind them. But when others offended a public official, they faced dire consequences. In March 1624 Captain Richard Quaile of Jamestown, a ship's captain who wrote a "controversial document," was stripped of his command and fined. His sword was broken and replaced with an axe, the symbol of a carpenter. While this reduction in status may have been psychologically and economically painful, it paled in comparison to the physical pain that the courts inflicted; Quaile had his ears nailed to the pillory in the market place. When Edward Sharples, clerk of the Governor's Council, was found guilty of sending unauthorized writings to the king, his ears too were nailed to the pillory and then cut off. Banished unarmed from Jamestown Island, he became an indentured servant for seven years. Richard Barnes, who criticized the governor, received especially severe punishment. He had both arms broken and his tongue bored through with a sharp instrument. A gauntlet of 40 men butted and kicked him out of the fort at Jamestown. For the crime of claiming that a man had been wrongfully accused, Peter Martin was "whipped from the fort to the gallows and then back again" then "set upon the pillory" where he lost one of his ears. Although he had just completed his term of indenture, he was required to serve another seven years.

As the colony's labor shortage worsened, sentences involving servitude became increasingly common. Often the wrongdoers ended up serving the governor or a member of his Council, the same men who handed down the sentence. A survey of Jamestown's legal record reveals that a promise, once given, had to be kept. Mrs. Jane Kingsmill overheard her neighbor's maidservant, Eleanor Sprage (Spradd), pledge to marry Robert Marshall. But before the couple's marriage bans could be posted in the parish church, as required by law, Eleanor became engaged to another and thus ran afoul of societal expectations. The coquettish girl was scolded publicly and made to apologize to her fellow parishioners. On another occasion, a local minister, at least according to rumor, intended to lure away Mara, the 12-year-old orphan of Richard Buck. Although witnesses described her as slow-witted, Mara was a young heiress at a time when females (especially wealthy ones) were scarce and never remained single for long. The Quarter Court dismissed the allegations against the clergyman whose brother, incidentally, sat as a justice.

Other colonists brought suit over economic broken promises. John Johnson of Jamestown Island, found guilty of breach of contract, had to repair the house of his neighbor, the late Ensign William Spence. Disagreements between servants and their masters sometimes reached the Quarter Court, usually because one or both parties failed to live up to contractual obligations. In 1624 when Captain John Harvey refused to produce ex-servant William Mutch's "freedom dues" (the corn and clothing usually given to newly freed servants) and Mutch made a scornful remark, Harvey brought the argument to a close by clubbing him "over ye pate with his truncheon," a short stick. Disputes over unpaid debts were commonplace; John Haule and Thomas Passmoure, for example, took their dispute over a debt to court.

Colonists occasionally turned to the Quarter Court to legitimatize leases, confirm a real estate transaction, probate wills and, whenever orphaned children were involved, appoint guardians to provide them with care and manage their property.

Not surprisingly, disputes often involved livestock. Two residents accused a neighbor of allowing his swine to uproot their vegetable gardens. Cases, on occasion, revolved around the ownership of cattle, which generally roamed at large and bore earmarks. In 1623 two Jamestown Island men, laborer Daniel Frank (Francke) and gunsmith George Clarke, stood accused of stealing a calf from Governor Yeardley. Clarke, who claimed that Frank had killed the calf, admitted helping him butcher it. Further investigation revealed that calf-stealing was not Frank's first crime. He previously had stolen several items from Jamestown's provost marshall, Randall Smallwood. The court sentenced both of the accused to death but offered Clarke a reprieve, perhaps because of his occupation.

Despite his own questionable activities, churchwarden Richard Kingsmill of Jamestown Island zealously reported fellow parishioners who got tipsy, swore, or went hunting on Sunday, all infractions of church law. The courts censured several local men for being drunk and disorderly at "unseasonable howres of the night." Others stood accused of less familiar offenses like "nightwalking" (venturing abroad late at night) and "nicknaming houses" (making defamatory remarks about their contemporaries, especially those in the upper ranks of society). Severe punishment awaited unmarried people who had sexual relations or indulged in inter-racial liaisons. Men and boys usually were whipped. Women and girls were shamed publicly, sometimes made to stand up in church, draped in a white sheet, and hold a wand, a symbol of lost innocence. One of the saddest cases heard by the Quarter Court involved two girls raped by a young male servant. Both children were "openly whipped in the fort at James City," receiving up to 40 lashes, and one girl's mother was flogged for failing to report the crime promptly. The rapist, meanwhile, was executed and his corpse put on display.

As most of the indentured servants who came to Virginia during the early seventeenth century were young and single and needed their masters' permission to marry, many unauthorized liaisons probably escaped detection.

The Quarter Court sometimes investigated deaths of unknown or suspicious cause. When four-year-old George Pope of Jamestown tumbled into an open well and drowned in 1625, an inquest revealed that Margaret Osborne, who took care of the child, often sent him to fetch water, which he scooped up with a dish and poured into a small barrel. Five-year-old Christopher Stokes, a neighbor, testified that George, on his last day, knelt with a dish "and the water beinge muddy" poured it out. When he leaned forward again, he fell in. This case, besides shedding light on the Pope youngster's premature death, revealed that nearly twenty years after European settlement was planted on Jamestown Island, its inhabitants still consumed murky and impure water.

Court records show that crime cut through all ranks of society. Dr. John Pott, a Jamestown resident, physician, and one-time governor, was convicted of cattle-rustling, a capital offense. Censured, Pott's final punishment awaited advice from the king. Governor Harvey wrote that Pott "was the only physician in the colony, skilled in epidemical diseases" and recommended leniency. The king finally granted a pardon to Pott.

The Quarter Court also handed down decisions that affected the colony as a whole. For example, in 1624 every male head of household over the age of 20 was required to plant four mulberry trees and 20 vines and to enclose his garden. Every household had to plant an adequate amount of corn. No one could relocate from one plantation to another without official permission and all men had to keep their firearms in good working order. All vessels entering Virginia waters had to pause at Jamestown before going elsewhere. This not only facilitated the collection of import duties it also allowed government officials (many of whom were merchants) first access to the ships' cargoes.

Virginians' dependence upon tobacco as their principal money crop created complex economic problems. With alternating "booms" and "busts" in the market, authorities tried to control both the quality and quantity of tobacco produced in the colony. In 1628 settlers had to plant two acres of corn "for every head that worketh the land" but no more than 2,000 tobacco plants per household member. Plants had to be set at least 4 1/2 feet apart; only twelve leaves could be picked from each. Inspectors examined all tobacco shipped abroad. Even so, as the new storage warehouses built on the riverbanks indicated, tobacco already was a principal source of income for many colonists.

RELATIONS WITH THE AMERICAN INDIANS

Relations between colonists and the Virginia tribes remained strained and occasionally violent. Sporadic attacks on outlying plantations and on those foolish enough to venture out alone and unarmed sustained memories of the 1622 Indian uprising. In October 1626 local officials gave colonists six months to build palisades around their dwellings. Those inhabiting necks of land were ordered to cordon them off with a line of posts and planks. Again, officials paid lip-service to the idea of running a palisade across the James-York peninsula and staged retaliatory expeditions against the Indians. In April 1627, warned that the Indians would attack in the spring, the colonists were ordered to see that their houses were securely impaled.

On April 24, 1628, four Indians brought the governor a message from several men being detained at the Pamunkeys' stronghold. Enraged, the government declared that it would procure the captives' freedom without making "any peace or dishonorable treaty" with the Indians. When they did negotiate a formal peace agreement in August 1628, officials openly admitted that they would honor it only until they saw "a fit opportunity to break it." By January 1629 they had found their excuse. Because many settlers had been remiss in maintaining their own defenses, all formal treaties with the tribes were declared extinct. Instead, in

The Indians Attack. Painting by Sidney King. Courtesy of the National Park Service, Colonial National Historical Park.

order to prevent a second massacre, the government chose "to proclayme and maintayne enmity and warres with all the Indians of these partes." Thus, the peace treaty was not broken on account of any hostile act by the tribes but because some colonists failed to provide for their own defense. There was a moratorium on shooting or killing Indians until February 1629, after which time they were deemed "utter Enemies." When a lone Indian ventured into the colonized area before his people were informed that the treaty was null and void, he was sent home with word that the agreement had been set aside because they (the Indians) had failed to abide by it. After dissolution of the 1628 treaty, when Indians needed to confer with governing officials, they had to approach Jamestown through an "appoynted place, at Pasbehay," west of Jamestown Island.

The relentless encroachment of European settlement continually heightened tensions. In March 1629 each of the colony's loosely defined communities was assigned a military commander. A summer-long drought during 1632 withered the corn crop making trade with the Indians a matter of survival. The colonists, still regarding the Pamunkey and the Chickahominy Indians as "Irreconcilable enemies," entered into a harsh treaty with them in October. Early in 1633 a long palisade cordoned off the James-York peninsula and excluded all native inhabitants. Shortly thereafter expansion continued when a small settlement was established midway between College and Queens creeks, in what became known as the Middle Plantation, later the site of Williamsburg.

JAMESTOWN ISLAND IN 1629

Once again, in 1629, Captain John Smith provided a description of conditions in Virginia. Based on the accounts of several colonists he encountered in England, Smith reported that, despite the fact that everyone was preoccupied with growing tobacco, food, beverages, and livestock reportedly were abundant. Governor John Pott and two or three council members resided at Jamestown, where two brewhouses helped to quench the thirst of the colonists. Most of the island's woods were gone, replaced with gardens and pastures. Fruit—peaches, apples, apricots, and figs—was plentiful. Smith likened the scattered houses of Virginia's plantations to English country villages and said that, according to his informants, the colony lacked fortifications. Nonetheless, defense remained a concern, and many plantations west of Jamestown Island had palisades into which their well-armed inhabitants could retreat. Although Indians seldom were seen, their fires still glowed in the woods at night.

Cooper Manufacturing. Painting by Sidney King. Courtesy of the National Park Service, Colonial National Historical Park.

THE ESTABLISHMENT OF COUNTY GOVERNMENT

During the late 1620s and early 1630s, Virginia's rapidly expanding population led to a reorganization of local government. In 1634 the colony was subdivided into eight shires or counties, each of which had a court. By handling routine legal matters, local justices relieved the overloaded docket of the Quarter Court. Jamestown continued to serve as the colony's capital, but now also became the seat of James City County's newly formed government. Both local and official life revolved around the county seat and, with obvious common sense, the two levels of government found a variety of ways to cooperate and economize. Both the local justices and the Quarter Court convened in the same building. The clerk of the Quarter Court also served as James City County's clerk of court, although he carefully maintained separate records. Likewise, the local sheriff usually doubled as the assembly's sergeant-at-arms. At Jamestown, the Quarter Court shared a jail, pillory, whipping post, stocks, and ducking stool with the county court. A gallows near Pitch and Tar Swamp stood silently by as a grim reminder to all potential lawbreakers. Jamestown did, however, elect its own burgess to the colony's assembly, apart from those chosen to represent James City County.

In 1634 when Governor John Harvey appointed the first group of county court justices, he chose men already involved in public life. What a modern observer might describe as a "conflict of interest" failed to concern citizens of the seventeenth century. Most high-ranking officials held more than one political office at a time. A county justice might serve as a burgess, a member of the Governor's Council, a tobacco inspector, and a military leader. By monopolizing political power, these men typically enhanced their personal wealth and secured their family's position in society. For example, George Menefie, simultaneously a member of the Council of State, a burgess and James City's official merchant, amassed

Sir John Harvey

A Virginia Company patented John Harvey set sail for Virginia in 1624 to report on the colony for the Privy Council. He bought land in the New Towne area of Jamestown and, by 1628, was named Governor George Yeardley's successor.

Following instructions from King James I, Sir John encouraged the production of oils, potashes, and soap. By 1630, he was able to ship to England rapeseed, salt peter, potashes, and iron ore.

Relations became increasingly strained between Governor Harvey and his Council. Although his accomplishments included providing better defensive structures for Virginia and greatly encouraging grain production, he was recognized as a man who was unable to compromise and who verbally and sometimes physically abused his Council. In 1635, the Council arrested Harvey and prepared a petition outlining the charges against him. Harvey was sent back to England to answer to King Charles I.

In January 1637, Sir John returned to Virginia to be reinstated as Royal Governor. Once again, he alienated his Council and other citizens of Virginia. In 1638, Sir Francis Wyatt was appointed his successor. By late 1641, Sir John returned to England. His will, which was probated in 1650, stated that Virginia and her inhabitants owed him over 7000 pounds in back pay and debts.

Shipbuilding. Painting by Sidney King. Courtesy of the National Park Service, Colonial National Historical Park.

Agricultural Beginnings. Painting by Sidney King. Courtesy of the National Park Service, Colonial National Historical Park.

immense wealth and owned vast amounts of land.

Throughout the 1640s, local government became increasingly defined. Local court justices assumed responsibility for the creation and maintenance of public graveyards, for the care of roads, bridges, and ferries, and for the legal operation of taverns and mills. They tried most civil cases, probated wills, collected taxes and distributed arms and ammunition to the local militia. In short, by 1652 the county courts presided over most local civic affairs.

STRENGTHENING THE COLONY'S CAPITAL

During the 1630s Jamestown also experienced a physical transformation. In March 1631 Governor John Harvey and his Council informed British officials that the colony needed tradesmen—shipwrights, smiths, carpenters, tanners, and other skilled workers, especially those who made and laid brick. Harvey convinced English investors to support colonial industries including the production of potashes, soap ashes, rapeseed, pottery, and medicinals.

Tobacco continued to fuel the Virginia economy and encourage trade and commerce. In 1633 there were five tobacco inspection warehouses in the colony. The warehouse at Jamestown served planters within a vast territory that stretched from Weyanoke Point to Lawnes Creek.

Continuing a now well established pattern, incoming ships still landed first at Jamestown, where all transactions involving tobacco had to be conducted. Jamestown merchants and shopkeepers eagerly bartered for the best of each cargo. Commerce during the 1630s was brisk between Virginia and New Amsterdam (New York). David DeVries, a Dutch trader, visited Jamestown in 1633 and stayed at the residence of the governor, Sir John Harvey, where he mingled with other guests and sipped imported wine from a Venetian glass. Although Harvey complained that his was the only house at Jamestown in which visitors could be entertained, it was his own fault. Harvey chose to have the governing bodies meet in his own home, which he eventually sold to the government when he fell on hard times.

Of course, some amount of intrigue followed the expansion of local government and increased wealth. Governor Harvey's prickly personality and political leanings eventually led to his downfall. Known for his fiery temper, on one occasion Harvey attacked councilor Richard Stephens, knocking out some of his teeth. Harvey's fierce loyalty to the king sometimes led him to endorse policies that were detrimental to the colony's interests. His own Council turned against him and literally thrust him from office. Although Harvey managed to get reinstated as governor, ultimately officials in England sided with his opponents.

In February 1636, while the temporarily deposed John Harvey nurtured political support in England, the Assembly passed legislation to enhance Jamestown's development. Residents who agreed to erect a building were entitled to "a convenient portion of ground for housing and a garden plot." In fact, land left vacant for six months could be re-assigned to another and most of the Jamestown patents issued during the 1630s and 40s contained a six-month building requirement. In July 1638, when the Privy Council learned that the public storehouse at Jamestown had "gone to decay," they ordered the governor to "deal with some private persons to build others." Legislation for the "laying out of grounds for merchants, handicraftsmen, and tradesmen" in Jamestown was revived again and would-be builders were awarded land on a use-or-lose basis. It was perhaps such legislative incentives that led a mariner, several mer-

chants, a brick-maker, and others to claim Jamestown lots around this time.

Symbolically, a large warehouse was built close to the James River. By 1639, a reinstated Governor Harvey informed his superiors that twelve new dwellings and stores had been built at Jamestown and that Richard Kemp, the colony's secretary, had erected a brick house that was "the fairest ever known in this country for substance and uniformity." Others, according to Harvey, had "undertaken to build framed houses to beautify the place" and contributed toward the construction of a brick church and statehouse. "There was not one foote of ground," Harvey boasted, "for half a mile altogether by the rivers side in Jamestown but was taken up and undertaken to be built on." With the colony fully engaged in expansion, only by continuing to restrict commerce to one place (Jamestown), he argued, would merchants and tradesmen congregate in an urban setting.

Archaeologists have uncovered actual evidence of pottery making at Jamestown, near Governor Harvey's official residence and on the waterfront.

Harvey's glowing reports failed to reach England in time to save him from final political judgment. While the dispatches sailed across the Atlantic, Harvey's superiors removed him from office and chose a successor. The ex-governor's financial problems ultimately overwhelmed him, forcing him to sell off his real estate and personal belongings.

In 1639 in-coming governor Francis Wyatt was authorized to relocate the colony's capital, if the Council and

Jamestown Pottery. Photograph, courtesy of Bly Straube.

Assembly agreed. But by that time too much had been invested in improving Jamestown, and the Assembly reiterated their preference for Jamestown as "the chief town and residence of the Governor." Wyatt was allowed to erect a special building in which his Council could meet, perhaps a public building or "country house" on the north side of Back Street in the heart of the New Towne, near Secretary Kemp's dwelling.

NEW INCENTIVES TO DEVELOPMENT

Official support from England coupled with the local energies of the newest incoming governor, Sir William Berkeley, and activist legislation passed by the Assembly spurred even more local development. In 1641 the king instructed Berkeley to oversee construction of a statehouse. Berkeley, like his predecessor,

Portrait of Governor Sir William Berkeley. Courtesy of the Berkeley Will and Trust and the Jamestown-Yorktown Foundation.

Sir William Berkeley

In 1642, Sir William Berkeley arrived in Virginia as the new Royal Governor. He proved to be a popular and sympathetic leader, establishing forts and creating a reservation system to provide a buffer zone between the settlers and hostile tribes. He encouraged planters not to rely solely on tobacco, using his own estate—Green Spring—to experiment with such diverse crops as cotton, flax, hemp, and rice. He also produced glass, silk, and potash.

In 1649, King Charles I was beheaded during the Civil War led by Oliver Cromwell. Sir William refused to support the Commonwealth and was relieved of his commission. By 1660, Charles II was on the throne. Berkeley, recognized as a staunch Royalist, was appointed governor for a second time.

Unfortunately due to his age and ill health, he was no longer the flexible, charismatic leader who served Virginia so ably years before.

In 1676, Nathaniel Bacon emerged as leader of a large group of disgruntled colonists. In the conflict described as Bacon's Rebellion, Jamestown was captured and burned in September 1676. The rebels' triumph was short-lived. When Bacon died of the bloody flux, the rebellion dissolved.

Berkeley sought revenge for the burning of Jamestown and the looting of Green Spring. Rebels were subjected to imprisonment and execution, and their lands and properties were confiscated.

Commissioners from England arrived to restore order and investigate the causes of the rebellion. By the spring of 1677, Sir William resigned as governor and set sail to plead his cause before the King. He died before he was granted an audience.

was authorized to relocate the capital if the burgesses agreed. But again they insisted that Jamestown remain the seat of government and the governor's domicile. Legislation passed in March 1642 offered land for a house and a garden to anyone willing to build, prompting a flurry of small lot claims at the western end of the island. In 1643 renewed emphasis was placed upon promoting the community's development and settlers were authorized to keep land upon which they had "built decent houses" whether or not others held title.

Actions taken by the Assembly in 1643 demonstrate apparent approval of the tenure of Governor Berkeley. In March they gave him two houses and an orchard, property they had purchased from the heavily indebted John Harvey. When the onset of the English civil war interrupted the governor's official salary, the burgesses made sure Berkeley received compensation from locally generated taxes on tobacco, wheat, malt, pork, beef, poultry, butter, and other commodities. Shortly thereafter, Berkeley patented approximately 1,000 acres at Green Spring (directly behind the Governor's Land) and made plans to develop his new acreage into a manor plantation. In February 1645 Richard Kemp informed Berkeley, who was then in England, that construction of his brick house at Green Spring was progressing well, but "that at towne for want of materials is yet no higher than ye first storye above ye cellar." It was likely around this time that Berkeley erected a three-unit brick rowhouse west of the parish church in Jamestown.

During the 1640s the Virginia economy showed signs of diversification. When Virginians began cultivating flax, the colony's governing officials decided to build a couple of public flaxhouses at Jamestown. There two children from each county could be taught how to process raw fiber into fabric. And twice during the decade officials extended invitations to the Dutch to increase trade in Virginia. The Dutch apparently responded positively. In 1648 one man said "at last Christmas we had trading here [at Jamestown] ten ships from London, two from Bristoll, twelve Hollanders, and seven from New England."

VIRGINIA AT MID-CENTURY

One description of life in Virginia, written in 1649, rivals the effusive promotional literature published earlier in the century. Evidence of prosperity existed everywhere. The colonists had plenty of barley and excellent malt and generally "brew their owne Beere, strong and good" although "they have Six publike Brewhouses." The author claimed that trade was brisk and that "above 30 saile of ships" bearing at least 700-800 mariners visited the colony annually. Virginia reportedly offered excellent opportunities to turners, potters, and coopers "to make all kind of earthen and wooden Vessels," to sawyers, carpenters, tile-makers, boatwrights, tailors, shoemakers, tanners, and fishermen. There was an abundance of ore for smelting iron.

In 1650 John Stirring prepared a more balanced account of life in Jamestown. According to Stirring, "two or three bru [brew] houses" formerly at Jamestown went out of business because customers refused to pay their bills. That may have been the fate of Captain John Moon of Isle of Wight County, proprietor of a Jamestown brewhouse, or the owner of Brewers Point in the western end of the island. Stirring agreed, however, that artisans and tradesmen, including turners and potters, could make an excellent living in Virginia. In fact, records show that Edward Challis owned a lot in the extreme western end of Jamestown Island near the isthmus and that he had a pottery kiln on a parcel he leased within the Governor's Land.

As the colony's official port of entry, Jamestown continued as the hub of Virginia's foreign and domestic trade. In light of earlier efforts to encourage trade with the Dutch, a navigation act imposed by the English government at midcentury forbidding importation of goods in foreign ships was enormously unpopular in Virginia. Clearly, the colonial market had captured the attention of merchants in England. A list of goods sent to Virginia by London merchant John Bland in May 1644 reveals that his cargo included everything from housewares and clothing to ammunition, tools, and alcoholic beverages. It is easy to imagine people crowding around the wharves at Jamestown to watch ships unload and catch up on the latest news.

A 1649 law designated the entire western end of Jamestown Island (from

Orchard Run to Sandy Bay) as an official market place. The area was open for business from 8 A.M. to 6 P.M. each Wednesday and Saturday. A special clerk recorded all transactions that occurred there making them legally binding. Within this ample area, merchants and vendors haggled with customers over produce, meat, and livestock. There they exchanged tobacco for imported goods. Evidently successful, this concept of creating special trading zones was expanded in 1655 when the Assembly authorized each of Virginia's counties to establish one or two markets that extended a mile or so along both sides of a navigable waterway.

By the mid-seventeenth century, settlement was well established throughout Tidewater Virginia east of the fall line, and across the Chesapeake Bay on the Eastern Shore. The colony's mortality rate had begun to level off, and by 1649 there were an estimated 10,000 inhabitants of European origin. The colony not only had managed to survive, it was gaining in momentum.

THE EVOLVING ROLE OF GOVERNMENT

An expansion of representative government in Virginia paralleled economic growth, owing to the Crown's failure to interfere with the growing independence of the colonists. The colony's assembly, through trial and error, slowly acquired a variety of rights, at times enjoying more power than its counterpart in England. By 1643 Virginia's Grand Assembly had become bicameral; the burgesses convened apart from the governor and Council, but both bodies worked closely with local officials to solve whatever problems arose.

CONTACT WITH THE INDIANS

Even interaction between colonists and natives increased. Settlers were encouraged to take Indian children into their homes and rear them as Christians. Natives (both young and old) became servants in planter households. This sometimes generated ill feeling, for tribal leaders also faced a shortage of workers. Although selling firearms to Indians remained illegal, other trade restrictions were eased somewhat. In 1641 Walter Chiles of Jamestown and three others were granted the right to explore the territory beyond the head of the Appomattox River. They hoped to establish trade with the Indians and to discover potentially marketable commodities.

Although a new treaty was signed with the Indians in April 1642, steady growth in the colony's population, accompanied by increased encroachment upon native lands, inevitably strained relationships once again. This time the explosion occurred on April 18, 1644, when a second major Indian uprising claimed the lives of between 400 and 500 settlers. Colonists suspected that Opechancanough, who they referred to as the "Bloody Monster," again led the attacks. Settlers along the upper reaches of the York River and on the lower side of the James, near the Nansemond River, bore the brunt of the violence.

In the aftermath, April 18, like March 22, 1622, was designated a holy day in commemoration of the massacre. The Grand Assembly resolved to "forever abandon all formes of peace" with the Indians and "root out those which have in any way had their hand in the shedding of our blood." Retaliatory expeditions unapologetically were intended to extirpate the Indians. Commander-in-Chief William Claiborne led a large, well-equipped army against the Pamunkey Indians, destroying their villages and cornfields. The Indians simply faded into the forest.

But, by February 1645, Richard Kemp informed Governor Berkeley that the colonists were running hazardously low on powder and shot. Shortages forced the Assembly to adopt a strategy that required fewer armed men assigned to newly constructed forts or surveillance points on the frontier. Officials identified three critical, remote locations and carpenters and other workers were pressed

The paramount chief, Opechancanough, slain at Jamestown. Courtesy of the National Park Service, Colonial National Historical Park.

into service. John Rolfe and Pocahontas's son, Thomas, built one of the forts in exchange for the land upon which it stood. In 1646 a fourth military outpost was constructed. But by that date, governing officials realized that it would be impossible to eradicate the elusive Indians. Instead, they sent out an expedition to take Opechancanough dead or alive. Governor Berkeley, upon learning that the aged chief had been sighted, rallied a party of armed horsemen and captured him. While jailed in Jamestown, Opechancanough was murdered by a soldier who shot him in the back. Opechancanough's death heralded the demise of the Powhatan empire and aided the increasing popularity of Governor Berkeley, now the "darling of the people."

In October 1646, Necotowance, immediate successor to Opechancanough, concluded a formal peace treaty with the Virginia government. The Indians agreed to humiliating terms. Each year they would pay an annual tribute to the Crown's representatives. The Virginia governor gained the right to appoint or confirm their leaders. They consented to withdraw from the James-York peninsula, inland as far as the fall line, and to abandon their land on the south side of the James, south to the Blackwater River. All natives entering the ceded territory could be slain lawfully, unless garbed in "a coate of striped stuff," worn by official messengers as a badge of safe conduct. Indian trade was restricted to the forts built on the Appomattox and Pamunkey rivers, where the special coats were kept when not in use. In return for these concessions, the Virginia government agreed to protect the tributary Indians from their enemies.

In March 1648 Necotowance and "five more petty kings attending him" came to Jamestown to deliver the first tribute of 20 beaver skins. But predictably, many natives at first failed to understand or accept the terms of the treaty or the necessity of wearing a striped coat when entering the ceded territory. According to a 1649 account, Necotowance reportedly said "My countrymen tell me I am a liar when I tell them the English will kill you if you goe into their bounds." Some paid the highest price for their skepticism and were shot.

Three native leaders, however, whose lands were engulfed by the rapidly expanding frontier, requested and received 5,000-acre tracts in compensation. In 1652 the Assembly agreed that "all the Indians of the collonye shall hold and keep those seats of land that they now have." They forbade settlers from encroaching on the natives' acreage. "Wrongs done to the Indians in taking away their lands," argued the burgesses, often had driven them "to attempt some Desperate course." The concept of creating Indian preserves or reservations in Virginia began to germinate. As tensions eased the settlers and their Indian neighbors again began to intermingle.

CLASS DIFFERENCES EMERGE

As the seventeenth century progressed and the colony's population increased, social and political distinctions between the classes became more apparent. Virginia became a distinctly stratified society. The governor and his councilors, who held the colony's top posts and shared some of their power with members of the Assembly, occupied the pinnacle of Virginia society. Despite expansion in the colony's territory and its population, the established ruling families and their kin tightened their grip on power and dominated Virginia's government. Some new arrivals with money and good political connections entered this tightly guarded sphere of influence.

Below the burgesses were county justices of the peace and other local officials. Somewhere between the top and bottom rungs of the socio-economic ladder were Virginians with landholdings of modest size. They were the middling farmers, skilled workers, and others with a limited but adequate amount of disposable income. Near the bottom were the lesser planters and landless freedmen. Servants who fulfilled their terms of indenture often sought to procure land of their own, but most lacked the means to do so. This led to a growing number of landless freedmen who leased land from larger planters. Some simply became transients.

Ethnic minorities, blacks, and Indians, with limited legal rights and diminishing opportunities for advancement, sank into the lowest level of the hierarchy.

❖

Chapter 4

❖

GROWING PAINS

CIVIL WAR IN ENGLAND

Even before England became embroiled in a bloody civil war, tensions between the Royalists (the monarchy's supporters) and the Roundheads (those who backed Parliament) spilled over upon the colonies. Virginians generally sided with the monarchy and in January 1649, when King Charles I was beheaded, the Assembly declared it treasonous to question Charles II's right of succession. Governor William Berkeley, fiercely loyal to the Crown, opened his home to Royalists who fled to Virginia. When the Roundheads prevailed, they hardly could tolerate Virginia's attitude and sent a fleet to assert their authority. In April 1652 Governor Berkeley, who had held office since 1641, stepped down. As he surrendered the colony, he signed a document that clarified its relationship with the mother country.

The new government recognized the colony's charter and the legality of its land patents. Virginians retained rights as citizens of the new Commonwealth of England. The Assembly continued to conduct business as usual although any laws that they passed had to be in keeping with those approved by Parliament. Virginians could trade freely. No taxes, customs, or imposts could be imposed upon them without their Assembly's consent. But the colonists did surrender all publicly owned arms and ammunition and Berkeley and his councilors had to subscribe to the articles of surrender or leave Virginia within a year.

CONSOLIDATION AND EXPANSION

Berkeley decided to stay. He sold his three-bay brick rowhouse at Jamestown, conveying one unit to Richard Bennett, the new governor. He sold another unit to Thomas Woodhouse, a tavern-keeper who sometimes hosted the Quarter

Portrait of King Charles I. Courtesy of the Colonial Williamsburg Foundation.

Surrender at Jamestown. Courtesy of the National Park Service, Colonial National Historical Park.

Court and Assembly, and the third to Francis Moryson, one-time councilor and Speaker of the Assembly. Berkeley then retired to Green Spring, where he channeled his considerable energies into agricultural experimentation and accumulation of additional land.

Like the ex-governor, many other Virginians turned their attention to consolidation of property and wealth. Several waterfront lots in Jamestown's New Towne changed hands during the mid-1650s and, in the 1660s, Thomas Woodhouse acquired a one-acre lot to the west of Orchard Run where a three-bay rowhouse later was built overlooking the James River.

The ruins of this rowhouse (on APVA property) are known as the Ludwell Statehouse Group. Thomas and Philip Ludwell owned units in the structure, and one or more bays in other parts of the building served as the colony's statehouse as did other structures in Jamestown. Governor Berkeley built three of the structure's bays.

New patents were issued for land in the extreme eastern and western ends of Jamestown Island. In 1652 Edward Travis, who wed the daughter and heir of Ancient Planter John Johnson, patented nearly 200 acres near Black Point. He consolidated several small farmsteads and acquired new land, expanding his holdings to 326 acres. By 1677 Travis owned 550 acres and, by the close of the eighteenth century, the Travis family owned over 800 acres in the eastern end of Jamestown Island and two or more town lots.

In the extreme western end of Jamestown Island, near the isthmus that led to the mainland, John Baldwin patented a tract in 1656 that adjoined the location of Governor Berkeley's brick rowhouse. A quarter century later, William Sherwood bought Baldwin's land and during the 1680s and 1690s amassed much of the land in the western end of Jamestown Island. Sherwood, a practicing attorney with friends among the socially and politically elite, married the widow of Richard James, a well-to-do merchant, and moved into her home. In 1680, after fire destroyed the James residence, Sherwood purchased a one-acre lot in New Towne and built a new brick house. In time, Sherwood acquired nearly 200 acres of land that abutted the Back River, in time amassing nearly 430 acres in the western and south-central portions of Jamestown Island. After Sherwood's death, his widow Rachel, married Edward Jaquelin, whose son-in-law eventually consolidated over 900 acres into what became known as the Ambler plantation.

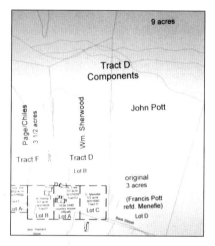

William Sherwood constructed his dwelling where the "country house," a government-owned building, formerly stood. Drawing by Christina A. Kiddle and Heather M. Harvey. Courtesy of the Colonial Williamsburg Foundation.

More generally, settlement continued in every direction as settlers cleared forested lands for agriculture. Small and middling farmsteads dotted Tidewater Virginia interspersed with the larger plantations of the well-to-do, who typically monopolized local political power.

RELIGIOUS INTOLERANCE

But not all was well. Religious intolerance pervaded society in both colony and mother country. Hatred and fear stalked anyone with religious beliefs different from the state established church. During the late 1650s, under Governor Samuel Mathews, three Quakers were brought before the General Court. One was whipped and the others banished from the colony. Because officials feared that the Quakers would attempt to make converts while jailed, they were deprived of all writing materials and communication with others. In 1661 and 1662 Quaker George Wilson was jailed at Jamestown and "chained to an Indian . . . in prison for murder." Wilson said that the jailer "had our legs on one bolt made fast to a post with an ox chain." Quaker preachers Josiah Cole and Thomas Thurston, also incarcerated at Jamestown, described the jail as "a dirty

dungeon where we have not the benefit to do what nature requireth, nor so much air to blow in at a window, but close made up with brick and lime."

EXPANSION AND INDIANS

As settlement expanded, the colonists' disregard for Indian rights led to persistent unrest. Governing officials realized that conflict over land precipitated most disputes and they continued to set aside acreage as tribal lands. But as land-hungry planters ventured into the Middle Peninsula, the Northern Neck, and the territory west of the fall line, they paid little heed when they intruded on acreage assigned to the Indians. Some brazenly settled within the natives' preserves while others tried to trick Indians into selling their land. Homesteads of covetous planters encircled Indian preserves, reducing land available for hunting and foraging. Native populations dwindled as the number of settlers increased. Despite public policy, even high-ranking officials like Sir Thomas Lunsford, a member of the Council of State, sometimes circumvented the law and claimed native lands.

Newly enacted laws reflected the strained colonial/Indian relations. A 1656 law required Indians to carry a pass or ticket whenever they wanted to hunt, fish, or forage within the colonized area. A 1662 law made them wear silver or copper badges, inscribed with their tribe's name, whenever they entered the territory inhabited by the colonists. Special markets for Indian trade were established although some trading probably occurred at Jamestown when the tributary Indians visited to pay their annual tribute.

In spite of these mutual suspicions, Virginia's tributary Indians, on occasion, served as military allies. In March 1656 Pamunkey and Chickahominy warriors sided with the colonists against 600 to 700 hostile natives who attacked homesteads near the falls of the James River. This conflict, the Battle of Bloody Run, claimed the life of the Pamunkey Indian leader, Totopotomoy.

PROMOTING ECONOMIC DEVELOPMENT

By May 1660, when word reached Virginia that the monarchy had been restored and that King Charles II had ascended to the throne, celebrants marked the occasion with trumpeting, gunfire, and drinking; one man received payment for more than 200 gallons of hard cider consumed by Jamestown merrymakers.

Sir William Berkeley, elected governor in March 1659, sailed to England to promote Virginia's economic interests with the newly formed Restoration government. He lobbied against the Navigation Acts that regulated colonial trade, asserting that England's best hope for economic supremacy lay in making Virginia the keystone of the empire. He also claimed that a shortage of skilled workers kept the colony from achieving its true economic worth. Berkeley himself showcased Virginia's economic potential. When he returned to Virginia, he experimented with potash, flax, hemp, silk, and wine at Green Spring, and turned his attention to the production of glass, earthenware, and salt. In 1663 he sent to England a ton of potash and enough black walnut lumber to wainscot several rooms. He pronounced the wine that he produced as good as any that "ever came out of Italy" and offered to send a hogshead of it to a friend at court.

But despite Berkeley's attempts to promote Virginia's economic development, Charles II paid little heed. Others had his ear and public policy actually harmed the colonists' interests. When, for example, the king confirmed title to the Northern Neck, the territory between the Potomac and Rappahannock Rivers, to court favorites, he dampened colonial enthusiasm for expansion.

LEGAL EVOLUTION

Amidst so much political and economic activity, Virginia's legal code evolved as well. Early in 1652 land on the lower side of the James River became Surry County, reducing James City's representation in the colony's assembly and decreasing its tax base. Beginning in 1661 each county sent only two burgesses to the Assembly although Jamestown, which had always had its own burgess, retained its ancient right to representation. A year later, when the Assembly formally adopted English common law, a new legal code regulated local elections, set the fees public officials could charge, and established local court procedures. Every county seat had to have a pillory, stocks, and whipping post near the courthouse as well as a ducking stool. The county court convened in Jamestown on the sixth day of every month, Sundays excepted, and its justices attended until each session had been completed. Plaintiffs and defendants had to summarize their cases in writing and were guaranteed the right to trial by jury. A litigant could appeal the county court's decision to the General Court, which was formerly known as the Quarter Court.

People flocked to Jamestown on court days, especially when the General Court was in session. Court cases often provided welcome diversion from mundane events and records of court proceedings provide snapshots of Jamestown society. Hubert Farrell, for example, found guilty of "most wickedly and maliciously scandalizing, abusing and defaming" Tabitha Bowler, filed an appeal with the General Court. He lost, was fined, and was forced to apologize. He also had to post a bond guaranteeing his good behavior because the "Scandall" was "Soe High and Soe Unjust" that it permanently damaged Bowler's reputation. In other court action, when Secretary Thomas Ludwell complained about the verbal abuse he had received from Giles Bland, Bland was promptly arrested and detained until he posted a large bond. In 1665 an English sea captain, William Whiting, stood trial for piracy. While in jail he shared space with the Indians he allegedly seized from the Spanish. According to court records, leaders of tributary Indian tribes sometimes came to Jamestown to seek justice from the General Court. And, shortly after the local sheriff detained a member of the General Court, anyone who came to Jamestown five days before or after the General

The Course of Justice. Courtesy of Dover Publications.

Court or Assembly convened was declared immune to arrest.

Some of the laws enacted in 1662 had little to do with rights and justice. Instead they focused on strengthening Virginia's economy and encouraging certain types of industry. County officials received flax seed and, in turn, offered it for sale. Those who raised and processed flax and wove it into cloth earned a bounty. New laws offered similar bonuses to those who planted mulberry trees or built ships. Each county had to have a public tannery and a weaver's workshop or face a penalty. While the law is clear, records are silent on effectiveness. The number and location of any industrial enterprises that resulted remains uncertain.

Because Virginia, like other colonies, continued to depend heavily on river and water-borne commerce, both the Assembly and the courts frequently addressed navigational concerns. By law all incoming ships had to pause at Point Comfort, pay duties, and present their manifests. They then proceeded to Jamestown to obtain trading licenses. Thus, Jamestown's inhabitants continued to have first access to newly imported goods, servants, and slaves. Legislation enacted in September 1663 indicated that the riverbank had become cluttered and even dangerous. The new law required townspeople to pull up all of the stakes "of the old wharfs about the town" which were "soe prejudicial and dangerous to boats landing." Further, they were enjoined "not to build new ones in the face of the town." This suggests that decrepit docks then protruded from a number of Jamestown's waterfront lots, traditionally the commercial district.

Officials showed the seriousness of their intent when they fined New Towne lot owner John Barber and two others for having "erected wharfs in the Face of the Town," contrary to law.

CHANGING THE FACE OF JAMESTOWN

In September 1662 the Privy Council, as the king's agent, ordered Governor Berkeley to see that towns were built on each of the colony's rivers, beginning with the James. So as not to be ignored, the Privy Council addressed Berkeley directly. "Give good example yourself," they told Berkeley, "by building some houses there, which will in a short time turn to profit." Further, the king would be very pleased, they suggested, if each of the colony's councilors also "build one or more houses there." In any event, they demanded a full account of who built what.

Although it is uncertain how many new houses were erected in Jamestown as a result of this official impetus to build, archaeologists uncovered the remains of numerous structures that conform with the 1662 standards and date to the 1660s. One was a three-bay rowhouse that stood close to the banks of the James. Others abutted Back Street, and some were close to the church. Archaeologists believe that a four-bay brick rowhouse erected between the Pitch and Tar Swamp and the common road dates to this period. Historical records reveal that the government built two of the four units while private individuals built the others.

Just three months later the Assembly also passed laws supporting new construction that promised to revitalize and enhance Jamestown itself. The government declared its intent to underwrite the cost of 32 brick houses, each to measure 20 feet by 40 feet with walls 18 feet high. Slate or tile would cover the roofs. These new houses were to be built side-by-side in a square or other pattern that Governor Berkeley deemed appropriate. No additional frame structures could be constructed in Jamestown, and older ones could not be repaired. Each of Virginia's 17 counties was instructed to erect a house, and by autumn 1663 four counties had complied. In addition to these publicly supported houses, the Assembly voted to reimburse private citizens who constructed one or more of the prototypical brick houses and to award them the lots upon which their buildings stood. A brick house built by Colonel Thomas Swann became a popular tavern. Situated in the heart of town, near the statehouse, it served the public for two or more decades.

With so much activity, Thomas Ludwell confidently informed English officials in April 1665 that the colonists had "begun a town of brick and have already built enough to accommodate the publique affairs of ye country." He reported construction of "a factory [retail building] for merchants," and added that flax, silk, potashes, and English grains were being produced along with small naval vessels useful in trading with neighboring colonies. During the 1660s one writer estimated that Jamestown had approximately 20 houses. But historian Robert Beverley, whose father was an active member of the Berkeley administration, claimed that most of the new buildings soon "were converted into Houses of Entertainment."

Perhaps in response to a similar observation that "all our laws [are] being made, and our judgements being given, in alehouses," the Assembly authorized Berkeley to build a statehouse to accommodate the General Court and the Assembly. The law set workmen's wages and created public levies to cover construction costs. Since all of the tobacco grown in James City County and two neighboring localities had to be processed for shipping by the proprietors of Jamestown's storehouses, tax revenues flowed freely into the communities' coffers.

In 1668 James City County officials further enhanced local facilities by converting one of the publicly funded brick houses into a jail. They chose a unit in a long brick rowhouse between the common road and Pitch and Tar Swamp.

WAR

In 1665 the Second Anglo-Dutch War broke out between England and Holland. When Governor William Berkeley received word of the war in early June 1665, he readied the colony's defenses. He told all militia units to expect an invasion. The colony planned to erect battery platforms and lines for small shot at Jamestown and three other sites where trading vessels would congregate for protection. The ordnance at Point Comfort was hastily brought to Jamestown. But a critical shortage of munitions forced governing officials to change their course of action. In October 1665 they decided to build a fort at Jamestown "at a site the governor shall think most convenient" instead of the battery platforms agreed upon earlier. Militia units from James City and Surry Counties were pressed into service to build a fort of earth and wood.

In late March 1666, however, the king intervened. Again swayed by influential English merchants, he ordered Berkeley to construct a fort at Point Comfort. Although Virginia officials realized invading ships could easily sail upriver beyond cannon range, they dutifully yielded to the orders of their monarch and initiated construction at the down-river location. In early July a Dutch man-of-war sailed into Hampton Roads, captured two ships and threatened other damage, prompting Berkeley to ask the king for two frigates to patrol the bay. Now supported by evidence of its deficiencies, Berkeley ordered Point Comfort abandoned. The garrison buried their cannon and withdrew. Later, the governor and his Council sent word to England that they had "designed a fort at James Town in the center of the country" and planned to install 14 great guns there. Secretary of State Thomas Ludwell reported that the colony had enough money to build one fort, allowing English officials to infer the fate of the Point Comfort fort.

DISASTER IN 1667

Natural disaster and the Dutch both struck Jamestown with a vengeance in 1667. In April a storm hit eastern Virginia that Thomas Ludwell said produced hail "as big as Turkey Eggs," destroyed the year's crops of nuts, fruit, and grain, broke "all the glass windowes and beat holes through the tiles of our houses," and "killed many young hogs and cattle." Then, on June 5, the Dutch sailed

Archeology at the Turf Fort. Courtesy of the Colonial Williamsburg Foundation.

boldly into the mouth of the James and captured or sank 20-some vessels heavy-laden with tobacco and awaiting the outbound tide. Mid-summer brought 40 days of rainy weather, drowning the season's crops. Finally, on August 27, a violent hurricane hovered over the region for 24 hours. Heavy rain and strong winds caused severe flooding that forced many families from their homes. Waves "impetuously" beat against the shores, ripping vessels from their moorings. Fences blew down releasing livestock that foraged through the year's corn, tobacco, and field crops. Demoralized and evidently somewhat chastened, the Assembly declared August 27 a day of annual fasting and atonement, attributing the hurricane to "the many sins of this country" that provoked "the anger of God Almighty against us."

In September 1667, when the Assembly convened at Jamestown, the burgesses, still smarting from the recent Dutch attack, revised their strategy and decided to build forts on each of Virginia's major rivers. Again, plans included a fort at Jamestown and special commissioners were appointed to oversee construction. Each fort's earthen walls were to be ten feet high, with a wall toward the river at least ten feet thick. By April 1668 the Jamestown fort stood ready to repel attacks, about the time the threat of a Dutch attack diminished.

NEW PROBLEMS WITH THE DUTCH

A resumption of hostilities with the Dutch in September 1672 (3rd Anglo-Dutch War, 1672-74) prompted governing officials to place local militia companies on alert and revived interest in construction of brick forts on all of the colony's major rivers. William Drummond and Major Theophilus Hone of Jamestown and Mathew Page of Archer's Hope were hired to build a 250-foot-long brick fort at Jamestown. Page died and, in April 1673, Drummond and Hone were ordered to complete the project or face severe punishment. Later, when military officials inspected the fort, they found that relatively little had been done and that the quality of the construction was "very bad and altogeth-

Portrait of Lady Frances Berkeley in her youth. Courtesy of the Museum of Early Southern Decorative Arts.

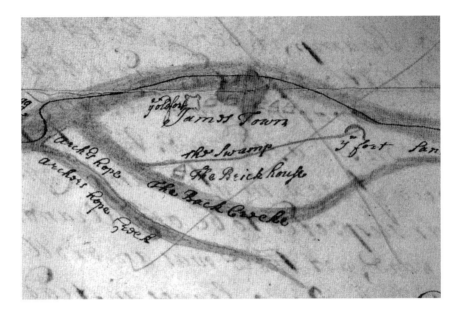

Untitled Map of Jamestown Island, done by the Reverand John Clayton in 1688. Courtesy of the Colonial Williamsburg Foundation.

er Insufficient." Despite the fort's defects, in July 1673, when the Dutch sailed into Hampton Roads again, a number of ships reached safety "above the fort" at Jamestown but not before 19 vessels anchored near Point Comfort had been burned or captured. In April 1674 the men who constructed the brick fort at Jamestown were told to "take Downe all such worke as is cracked and insufficient" and to mend its coping. Fines from court cases often funded maintenance of the brick fort and its weaponry.

In 1688 the Reverend John Clayton of James City Parish made a map of Jamestown Island showing both forts. The abandoned earthen fort of the 1660s (which Clayton termed "ye old fort" of earth) was located on the riverbank just west of Orchard Run. In Clayton's words, it was "a sort of Tetragone with something like Bastions at the four corners," built too far from the river's channel to be very effective. As to the brick structure built during the 1670s, Clayton said that it was "a silly sort of fort, . . . a Brick Wall in the shape of a Half-Moon" that was "little better than a blind Wall to shoot wild Ducks or Geese." His sketch of Jamestown Island indicated that the brick fort stood on the riverbank, in a swale between the church and the rowhouse known as the Ludwell Statehouse Group. Because it stood "in a vale," Clayton said its guns were likely to lodge their shot in the rising embankment. He commented that enemy ships would have to be almost on top of the fort before they came under its guns, and that if they fired a broadside, the fort's occupants would be thrown into utter confusion.

Clayton's map also showed buildings along the riverbank west of Orchard Run. At the rear of the island, a substantial brick house stood upon the west side of Kingsmill Creek's mouth, overlooking Back River.

GOVERNOR BERKELEY'S DECLINE

In April 1670, at age 64, Governor Berkeley married Frances Culpeper Stephens, the 36-year-old widow of Samuel Stephens, one-time governor of Albemarle or Carolina. By 1672 Berkeley had sold some property in Jamestown, and his new wife had disposed of a valuable Warwick County plantation that she had inherited from her former husband. This infusion of wealth made it possible for the Berkeleys to expand the Green Spring mansion significantly. In the autumn of 1674 the Grand Assembly confirmed Sir William Berkeley's title to his enlarged Green Spring plantation, noting that he "hath expended a great summe of money in building . . . upon the land." Personally comfortable, Berkeley continued to serve as governor, enhancing his reputation as a testy and arrogant leader very possessive of his privileges. In 1673, for example, he had Benjamin Eggleston hauled before the General Court because Eggleston had "presumptuously and impudently intrenched upon the perogative and abused the Authority of the Right Honorable Governor." Although the nature of Eggleston's offence remains unclear, he received 39 lashes at Jamestown's whipping post and a heavy fine. His father, Richard, owned nearly 2,300 acres adjoining Green Spring. The aging governor had flogged his neighbor's son. Worse was yet to come.

❖

Confrontation between Governor Sir William Berkeley and Nathaniel Bacon. Painting by Sidney King.
Courtesy of the National Park Service, Colonial National Historical Park.

CATALYSTS FOR CHANGE

THE TUMULT BEGINS

During the mid-1670s circumstances combined to create a crisis for Governor William Berkeley, now fractious and in failing health. Because the planter elite had solidified its power during his nearly 30 years in office, those outside the circle of privilege blamed him for many of the government's ills. Also, many people perceived political officials in general as opportunists who profited handsomely from performing duties that were a public trust. Personality conflicts among some of the colony's more volatile leaders added to the growing dissention. Giles Bland of Charles City County, for example, insulted Secretary Thomas Ludwell, who promptly called for his arrest. Bland responded by calling Ludwell "a Sonne of a whore, [a] mechannick fellow, puppy [puppet] and coward" and then challenged him to a duel. When Bland sent "a mutinous and scandalous letter" to Governor William Berkeley, forwarding a copy to England, he was thrown into jail.

These squabbles were symptoms not causes of the colony's troubles. Virginia planters chafed under the restraints of the Navigation Acts, which limited the sale of tobacco to England. Although Governor Berkeley urged Virginians to diversify the economy, few listened. Colonists in the Northern Neck worried about the legality of their land titles. Taxes soared. Stronger, warlike Indians inhabiting the interior attacked outlying plantations and the colony's native allies. In addition, as the Dutch had demonstrated, foreign invasion could cause considerable damage to trade. The scene was set for the tumultuous appearance of Nathaniel Bacon, Jr. The son of a wealthy English gentleman and Governor Berkeley's cousin by marriage, young Bacon earned a reputation as quick-witted, ambitious, and arrogant. Bacon's father withdrew his troublemaking son from

Cambridge University, gave him some money, and packed him off to Virginia where, presumably, he could cause less embarrassment. Shortly after he arrived, Bacon bought a plantation in Henrico County on the upper reaches of the James River. In March 1675 Governor Berkeley appointed him to the Council of State, of which his uncle, Colonel Nathaniel Bacon, was a member.

Indian unrest precipitated at least the appearance of crisis. In March 1676 Virginia's governing officials declared war on all natives implicated in recent attacks on frontier families and ordered construction of forts at nine sites near the heads of the colony's rivers. Fear led some on the outskirts of settlement to abandon their homesteads. Once again, men were pressed into service to garrison the forts. Public levies raised funds to buy supplies and military equipment. Many colonists, however, grumbled about paying for the forts, which they likened to expensive "mousetraps," useless against roving bands of hostile Indians.

THE REBELLION GETS UNDERWAY

After Indians attacked Bacon's plantation in the spring of 1676, he agreed to lead a retaliatory march. Governor Berkeley, upon learning of Bacon's plans, ordered him to report to Jamestown first. Bacon responded by demanding a commission to legitimize his pursuit of Indians and continued on his way. This incensed Berkeley, who declared Bacon a rebel, dismissed him from his council seat, and sent the militia after him. But it was too late. Bacon reached the colony's southern frontier ahead of the official militia. There, making no distinction between friend and foe, he attacked the Occoneechee, recent colonial allies against the Susquehannock. Bacon's Rebellion had begun.

As soon as Bacon returned home, he sailed for Jamestown accompanied by 50 armed men. He arrived on June 6 and, shielded by darkness, slipped ashore to confer with two of his more ardent supporters, William Drummond and innkeeper Richard Lawrence. When Bacon returned to his sloop, Sheriff Theophilus Hone arrested him and brought him before Governor Berkeley. Shortly thereafter, literally hundreds of Bacon's supporters streamed into Jamestown determined to rescue him. Bacon and Berkeley appeared to back away from additional confrontation. Bacon offered Berkeley a written apology. Berkeley accepted and restored Bacon to his council seat.

Evidently, Bacon simply had bartered for time. According to Jamestown resident William Sherwood, on June 22 Bacon and 500 supporters headed toward the capital again. Although Berkeley ordered "fower great Guns . . . drawn from ye fort to Sandy Bay," he ran out of time and faced Bacon's supporters without defense. The rebel leader marched into Jamestown and took control of the "ferry, River and fort." He then ordered his men to the statehouse where, at gunpoint, he again demanded a commission to fight the Indians. When Berkeley hesitated, Bacon's followers threatened to kill those who opposed him. With no choice, the governor granted Bacon his commission.

Flushed with power Bacon went further, insisting on political reforms as well. He forced the burgesses to expand Jamestown's corporate limits to include the entire island and gave qualified voters the right to enact local bylaws as long as they did not contradict the overarching rules of government. Then he struck another blow at the Indians, giving colonists the right to patent land set aside for the Indians, whether or not the natives had vacated it voluntarily.

On June 26, 1676, Governor Berkeley withdrew to Green Spring and tried to raise troops of his own. Since most planters hesitated to oppose Bacon, their ally against the Indians, the governor had little success and soon prudently withdrew to the Eastern Shore.

Meanwhile Bacon and his partisans roved the countryside trying to increase their ranks and gather ammunition and supplies. From his headquarters Bacon issued a "Declaration of the People," leveling charges against Berkeley, and a "Manifesto," justifying his own actions. He sent three ships after Berkeley hoping to surprise the governor again and place him under arrest. Perhaps to shore up his reputation as an Indian-fighter, Bacon also turned his wrath toward a convenient target, the Pamunkeys, a tributary tribe that recently had signed a peace treaty with the government. His men pursued the Pamunkeys into the Dragon Swamp where they killed men, women, and children indiscriminately, took captives, and plundered the Indians' goods.

Governor Berkeley, learning of Bacon's absence, rallied his own loyalists and, on September 7, returned to Jamestown. He offered a pardon to the 500 rebels garrisoned there and had a palisade built across the narrow isthmus that connected the island with the mainland. He then awaited the confrontation he considered inevitable when Bacon and his army returned.

As the Pamunkey expedition drew to a close, Bacon learned that his men had been unsuccessful in their attempt to capture Berkeley and that Jamestown again was under the governor's control. To swell his ranks, Bacon offered liberty to slaves and servants willing to join his army and set out for Jamestown, displaying his Indian captives along the way. On September 13, 1676, Bacon and his partisans pitched camp just west of Jamestown Island. He advanced onto the isthmus on horseback and had one of his men sound a trumpet. Bacon then raised and fired his carbine, but did not attack. Instead he sent some of his men to Green Spring to raid the governor's food supply while he constructed a "French work" or trench on the mainland side of the isthmus, close to Glasshouse Point. Bacon's fortifications consisted of a deep ditch fronted with a steep embankment of earth, trees, and brush. One eyewitness later estimated that the opposing fortifications stood only 100 to 150 paces apart.

The next day Bacon placed the wives of several loyalist leaders, including his own aunt, Elizabeth Kingsmill Bacon, upon the ramparts of the trench that faced Governor Berkeley's palisade. He also put his Pamunkey captives on display to demonstrate his prowess as an Indian fighter. Prodded to action,

Berkeley's loyalists made a sally against Bacon but fled so hastily from the rebels' withering gunfire that one wag likened them to "scholars goeing to schoole [who] went out with hevie harts but returned home with light heeles." Next, Bacon used his two cannon to bombard Jamestown, "playing some calls itt, that takes delight to see stately structures beated downe and Men blowne up into the aire like shuttle cocks." Merchant John White of Jamestown and at least four others lost their lives in the attacks. Outgunned, Berkeley and his supporters boarded a ship and again fled to safety on the Eastern Shore.

THE DESTRUCTION OF JAMESTOWN

Bacon entered the city on September 19, 1676, and put it to the torch. According to one eyewitness, as Berkeley's supporters retreated to safety they "saw with shame by night the flames of the town which they had so basely forsaken." In all, the conflagration destroyed an estimated 16 to 18 houses, along with the church and the statehouse. Richard Lawrence and William Drummond set their own dwellings ablaze but Drummond spirited many of Virginia's official records from the state-house sparing them from destruction.

The Burning of Jamestown. Courtesy of the National Park Service, Colonial National Historical Park.

Bacon withdrew to Green Spring where he drafted a protest against Governor Berkeley and asked his partisans to sign it. Some, heady with confidence and spoiling for a fight, plundered the estates of those loyal to Berkeley. Too late, Bacon tried to bring his men under control. The rebellion appeared poised to explode into an unruly mob when suddenly, on October 26, 1676, Bacon died of the "bloody flux." His successor, Joseph Ingram, lacked Bacon's charisma. He divided the dwindling rebel army into small bands that withdrew into the countryside, where they fortified themselves against assault.

THE REBELLION SUBSIDES

Governor Berkeley seized the initiative. During November and December his supporters hunted down and captured many of the rebels. On January 24, 1677, several of Bacon's followers appeared before a military tribunal convened at Green Spring. Convicted of treason and rebellion they received death sentences. A local woman recalled that some of the condemned men were "hanged at Bacon's Trench" near Glasshouse Point; others were executed at Green Spring. By July 1677 a total of 23 men had been put to death for their role in the uprising. But Berkeley's zeal for revenge went even further. He had his supporters seize the personal property of convicted or suspected rebels and bring it to Green Spring.

News of the rebellion prompted King Charles II to send three commissioners to investigate. Berry and Moryson arrived in late January 1677, and Herbert Jeffreys arrived on February 11 with a thousand royal troops and orders for Governor Berkeley's recall. They quickly learned that Bacon had died, that the rebellion had been quelled, and that Jamestown lay in ashes. Because the governor's residence at Green Spring was "very much ruined by the rebels," the commissioners stayed at Swann's Point, the Surry County home of Colonel Thomas Swann, a some-time Bacon supporter dubbed "ye great Toad" by detractors.

Damage reports catalogued the destruction. Berkeley claimed that his "houses [were] burnt in James City, his dwelling house at Green Spring almost ruined, his household goods and others of great value totally plundered." William Sherwood's stepson, Sheriff Theophilus Hone, Colonel Thomas Swann, Colonel Nathaniel Bacon and others also lost houses in the Jamestown fire. John Jeffreys reportedly lost 63 pipes of wine, some consumed by fire and some by Berkeley's supporters. Thomas Ludwell, who owned a dwelling in Jamestown and a nearby plantation, claimed that his "stock was utterly ruined and taken away by the late Rebells." His brother, Philip, said that Bacon's men had plundered him "of all within their Reach both without and within Doors besides my Books and papers to a considerable value."

As the days wore on the dialogue between Berkeley and the king's commissioners became increasingly terse, exacerbated by the aging governor's inability (or perhaps unwillingness) to transport and store food and ammunition for the king's troops. In mid-February, when they warned him that the king would take a dim view of his confiscating private property, Berkeley retorted that he had no knowledge of such seizures and had authorized none. He added, however, that his neighbors had stolen his goods and failed to return them.

When the Grand Assembly met at Green Spring, they passed 20 new legislative acts including four that pertained to Bacon's Rebellion. Those convicted of treason were obliged to forfeit their real estate and personal belongings. Other active participants in the rebellion were fined. Plundered goods were to be restored to their rightful owners, and those who had suffered significant losses had the right to sue for compensatory damages. The Assembly nullified the legislation Bacon had forced upon them and declared two new holy days: May 4, a day of fasting in repentance for the rebellion, and August 22, a day of thanksgiving to commemorate its end. Sheriff Theophilus Hone, whose rental home was destroyed when Jamestown burned, petitioned for the right to lease and rebuild two adjoining units of the brick rowhouse near Pitch and Tar Swamp.

In March 1677, when the surviving ringleaders of Bacon's Rebellion were tried at Green Spring, some were fined or subjected to other forms of censure, but nine more were sentenced to hang. Colonel Francis Moryson, one of the king's commissioners and a man Governor Berkeley had befriended during the Commonwealth period, asked Lady Frances Berkeley to intercede on behalf of a man accused of treason. She declined, stating that she would "rather have worn the canvas the Rebels threatened to make her glad of." On April 22, 1677, immediately prior to Sir William Berkeley's departure for England, the king's commissioners experienced a major affront. When the governor's coach transported them from Green Spring to Jamestown, the common hangman served as postillion. The outraged commissioners informed Berkeley that the incident was "an insult to the King's Great Seal" and said that they would report it to the monarch himself. Berkeley, however, claimed himself "innocent in this as the blessed Angels themselves" and said that he had sent his slave to be "racked, tortured or whipt till he confesses how this dire misfortune happened." But the commissioners had seen Lady Berkeley spying upon them "through a broken quarrel of glass to see how the show looked" and refused to accept the incident as accidental.

SIR WILLIAM BERKELEY'S EXODUS

Sir William Berkeley's departure for England ended the long string of death sentences even though Berkeley's most ardent supporters objected to Lieutenant Governor Herbert Jeffreys' more lenient attitude toward the rebels. Philip Ludwell I, known as a hothead, viewed Jeffreys' policies with disdain and accused him of perjury.

Apparently, Jeffreys intended to focus on more positive and practical action. In late May he and his Council discussed building or repairing a structure that could serve as a statehouse and finding a residence suitable for a governor. As the prison at Jamestown had been destroyed in the 1676 fire, several criminals had to be returned to county jails.

When Sir William Berkeley died in England in July 1677, a dominant personal influence passed from the pages of colonial history. Survived by his widow, Lady Frances, he left his Virginia landholdings including Green Spring to her care. She restored the mansion to habitable condition, hoping to rent it to future governors. In 1681 Thomas Lord Culpeper did so, as did his successor, Francis Howard (Lord Effingham), who arrived in 1686. During their terms in office the colony's assembly and the General Court convened several times at Green Spring.

RELATIONS WITH THE INDIANS

Despite the recent chaos of the rebellion, on May 29, 1677, yet another peace agreement was concluded with the colony's tributary Indians. In a colorful ceremony at Middle Plantation, Cockcoeske, Queen of the Pamunkeys, her young son, and several other native leaders knelt before Lieutenant Governor Herbert Jeffreys, "kissed the paper of peace" and then endorsed it with their signature marks. Afterward, guns were fired to commemorate the occasion, and the Indian leaders who had signed received special gifts. Cockcoeske, who was singled out for recognition because of her steadfast loyalty to the English, received a coronet, an ermine-trimmed robe, a white silk dress, and jewelry.

Silver pendant of the Queen of Pamunkey, inscribed with the royal coat of arms of King Charles II. Courtesy of the Virginia Department of Historic Resources and the Association for the Preservation of Virginia Antiquities.

Despite the new peace agreement, sporadic outbreaks of violence continued to plague the colony's frontier. Iroquois and Susquehannock Indians periodically swept down upon homesteads. In 1697 "flying armies" that consisted of a lieutenant and twelve horse soldiers were placed on constant guard at the head of the James, York, Rappahannock, and Potomac rivers, where they could watch over the fringes of the colony's frontiers. Tributary Indians sometimes served as guides. Only new peace agreements involving tribes beyond Virginia's borders eased frontier unrest.

Meanwhile, the tributary Indian tribes quarreled among themselves and from time to time asked the colonial government to intercede. As troubles often stemmed from unscrupulous trading practices, special markets were established in several places so that commerce could be controlled. And, to reduce ill feelings between Indians and whites, regulations described conditions of employment for Indian servants.

GROWTH AND URBANIZATION

King Charles II's interest in continuing development persisted. In 1680 Governor Thomas Culpeper informed the burgesses that the monarch wanted Virginia to have towns and ports like his other colonies. The Assembly responded by passing an act promoting development, trade, and manufacturing. Fifty acres of land in each of Virginia's 20 counties were designated official ports of entry; Jamestown was James City County's port town. All exports after January 1, 1681, and all imports (including slaves, English servants, and merchandise) after September

Wine bottle Seals from the Jamestown Museum Collection. Courtesy of the National Park Service, Colonial National Historical Park.

The Plight of the Enslaved. Courtesy of the Colonial Williamsburg Foundation.

29, 1681, were to be landed and sold at one of these ports of entry. Surveyors subdivided the towns into half-acre lots, which purchasers had to improve within a year or face forfeiture. The 1680 town act offered important incentives to would-be developers, fixing prices for the transportation and storage of goods in the official warehouses to be built in the ports. Skilled workers who set up shop in the towns received five years immunity from prosecution for bad debt.

Despite these incentives, most Virginia planters had little interest in urbanization. But at least four individuals (including two high-ranking officials) asked for the right to lease and rebuild units in the four-bay brick rowhouse that bordered Pitch and Tar Swamp and the common road. In reality, only merchant George Lee followed through, rebuilding the easternmost units, which, during the 1680s and 90s, accommodated the office of the General Court and meetings of the House of Burgesses.

In 1682 the king again ordered Culpeper to encourage development, adding that towns should be built on each of the colony's major rivers. Jamestown, "not only the most antient but the most convenient place for ye Metropolis of our said Colonie," was to be rebuilt as soon as possible. This prompted the community's landowners to ask the Assembly to define its corporate limits, which traditionally extended from Sandy Bay to Orchard Run and from the James River to Back Creek, encompassing far more than the 50 acres specified in the 1680 town act. They recommended that Jamestown's legal limits be expanded to include the entire island and that all vacant marshland be converted to common ownership. They also insisted that the sum set for the acquisition of town sites was inapplicable to Jamestown, where acreage was much more valuable and already contained buildings. Some Jamestown lot owners asked for the right to build storehouses, with the understanding that if they failed to do so, their land could be sold at a value assigned by the county court. Perhaps in response to the official interest in developing Jamestown, several new patents were issued during the 1680s and 90s for land in the western end of the island near the church. All but one of the patentees were high ranking officials.

On October 21, 1687, the Council of State decided to proclaim the king's "Declaration for Liberty of Conscience" in Jamestown. This so-called act of toleration permitted non-Anglican religious groups to assemble for worship and was announced "with the beat of the drum and the firing of two great guns and with all the joyfulness this colony is capable to express." The day held special meaning for those whose religious beliefs differed from Virginia's state church. Durand de Dauphine, a French Huguenot who visited the colony during the late 1680s actually considered bringing a group of Protestant refugees to Virginia where they now could enjoy a measure of religious freedom.

The Last Formal Statehouse at Jamestown. Conjectural drawing by
Cary Carson. Courtesy of the Colonial Williamsburg Foundation.

SEAT OF THE COLONY'S GOVERNMENT

Because Bacon's rebels destroyed the colony's statehouse, the House of
Burgesses, the Council of State, the General Court, and justices of the local
county court had to seek other accommodations. The burgesses convened at
Green Spring several times, but often met in Jamestown taverns or rented meeting space in private homes. Even after the Assembly hired Colonel Philip
Ludwell to restore the statehouse to usable condition in May 1684, the governor
and his Council continued to meet in William Sherwood's home. In February
1691 Henry Hartwell and William Edwards, Jamestown residents and justices of
the James City County court, asked the Council of State's permission to hold
monthly courts in the newly restored General Court facilities. They pointed out
that after Bacon's rebels destroyed the statehouse, the county had built a courthouse, which they shared with the General Court. The Council agreed, as long
as they maintained its windows and kept its plaster in good repair. In November
1693 three people received payment for repairs to the "extremely decayed and
rotten" General Courthouse and for digging a vault beneath a newly erected
powder house. The statehouse was repaired several times during the late 1690s,
and at least one of the offices in the building was enlarged and remodeled.

JAMESTOWN'S FINAL FLURRY

In 1691, when the Port Act reaffirmed and expanded the 1680 act, Jamestown was re-designated an official port of entry. Although the 1691 act gave rise to several new communities (including Yorktown), King William III and Queen Mary II sent word that Jamestown would remain the seat of government and they wanted every council member to build a house there. This produced a flurry of patenting and new construction along the waterfront.

Archeological Excavation of Structure 112. Courtesy of the Colonial Williamsburg Foundation.

DEFENDING THE COLONY'S CAPITAL

At the end of the century Jamestown came under attack on several fronts. When Lieutenant Governor Francis Nicholson, who held office from 1690 to 1692, arrived in Virginia, he inspected the colony's military defenses and found them weak. In 1693, after Lieutenant Governor Edmund Andros took office, a vaulted magazine and storehouse were built on the riverbank at Jamestown. Two years later, the 20-year-old fort was inspected and its brick found to be decayed. Because the Council believed that repairing it would be more costly than building a replacement, John Tullitt (Tullett) of Jamestown received payment for "beating down the Brick work & levelling the Fort," and another local man was hired to make "a platform for the great guns." The Reverend James Blair, an outspoken critic of Edmund Andros, in 1697 informed officials in England that Andros had

> . . . thrown away a great deal of money in raising [razing] an old fort at Jamestown, & in building a powder house, and in making a platform for 16 great guns there. . . . I never heard one man that pretended to understand anything of Fortification, that upon sight of these works, did not ridicule & condemn them as good for nothing but to spend money.

Blair stated that Andros' gun platform was so far above the town that it was useless and he added that the isolated and unprotected powder magazine would prove an easy target for an enemy. Two years later, the arms and ammunition in Jamestown's powder magazine were moved to Middle Plantation, and the fort's gunner was retired.

THE COLLEGE OF WILLIAM AND MARY

A more subtle threat to the capital began innocuously on February 8, 1693, when King William III and Queen Mary II granted a charter to the College of William and Mary to establish "a certain place of universal study, or perpetual college, for divinity, philosophy, languages and other good arts and sciences." The monarchs endowed the newly-created educational institution with 20,000 acres of land and public revenues (such as the duties upon exported furs, skins, tobacco, and imported liquors) earmarked for construction and support. In December 1693 a 330-acre tract of land in Middle Plantation was purchased as the site of the new college. By 1694 a grammar school had opened "in a little School-House" on its campus. A year later workmen laid the first bricks for the college's main building, and by 1697 the grammar school was "in a thriving way."

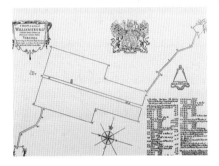

Boundaries of the City of Williamsburg, 1699. Courtesy of the Colonial Williamsburg Foundation.

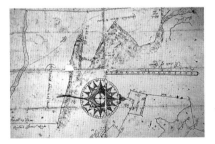

John Soane's plat of William Sherwood's land, 1681. Courtesy of the Colonial Williamsburg Foundation.

Within two years a small community, including a church, an ordinary, several stores, two mills, and a smith's shop had grown up near the college.

RELOCATING THE CAPITAL

On October 20, 1698, fire "broke out in a house adjoining the State-house, which in a very short time was wholly burnt, and also the prison." Arthur Jarvis, a convicted felon and burglar, jailed and awaiting execution, evidently set the blaze. Many of the public records were tossed from windows before flames completely engulfed the burning building. Afterward, the governor and Council continued to meet in the home of William Sherwood's widow, just as they had before the fire, and the General Court began convening there, too. John Tullett, who then occupied the eastern bay of the long rowhouse on Pitch and Tar Swamp, was asked to "repair and fit up" his dwelling to accommodate meetings of the Assembly.

Although some people reported that during the late 1690s Jamestown had 20 to 30 houses, then-Governor Francis Nicholson claimed that the old capital city was "reduced to so mean a condition that it cannot give entertainment to the people attending both a General Assembly and a General Court together." On May 1, 1699, students from the College of William and Mary urged the General Assembly to move the capital to Middle Plantation. The burgesses agreed and a month later voted to approve the move. Settlement had spread inland and now the government followed.

The Wren Building and the Capitol in Williamsburg as depicted on the Bodelian plate. Courtesy of the Colonial Williamsburg Foundation.

JAMESTOWN AT THE CLOSE OF THE CENTURY

Relocating the seat of the colony's government irrevocably changed the course of Jamestown's history. Its importance diminished almost immediately. Although some lot owners retained their property, plantations developed by the successors of William Sherwood and Edward Travis's heirs absorbed the bulk of the island's acreage.

Near the close of the seventeenth century, James City County surveyor John Soane made maps of Sherwood's landholdings at Jamestown. One shows the site of the "blockhouse hill," a slightly elevated piece of ground upon which Virginia's early colonists built a watchtower to maintain surveillance over the isthmus to Jamestown Island. Soane also mapped Sherwood's New Towne acreage and identified the site of his dwelling, which sometimes served as an interim seat of government.

❖

THE OLD CAPITAL IN TRANSITION

THE ECLIPSE CONTINUES

In 1700 the transition from old to new capital remained incomplete. The great men of several tributary Indian tribes trekked to Jamestown to meet with the governor and his Council and approximately 170 French Protestant refugees, having fled religious persecution in their homeland, landed. The Huguenots intended to establish a settlement on the upper reaches of the James River, but they arrived just as winter approached. Impoverished and unfamiliar with living conditions in the colony, they remained in the vicinity of Jamestown until the following year.

Nonetheless, by the close of 1700, the House of Burgesses and Council of State had begun meeting in Williamsburg at the College of William and Mary. In 1703, with construction of a new statehouse already underway in Williamsburg, the governor and Council received a surprising and certainly a troublesome message from Queen Anne—she wanted Jamestown to remain the seat of the colony's government. Cautiously, Virginia officials responded to the monarch that she and her predecessor had failed to disallow the legis-lation authorizing the move to Williamsburg. And, although the General Court continued to convene at Jamestown, the transition continued despite the queen's correspondence.

Since the James City County's court also continued to meet in Jamestown, the justices asked the House of Burgesses to allow them to use bricks from the old, burned-out statehouse to construct a new county courthouse. But roughly a decade later in 1715, some of James City County's justices apparently sought to leave Jamestown as well. They asked Lieutenant Governor Alexander Spotswood to make Williamsburg the seat of the county court. When a number

A View of Williamsburg's Historic Area. Courtesy of the Colonial Williamsburg Foundation.

of local citizens opposed the change, the burgesses appointed a committee to study the situation. George Marable, a James City County justice and Jamestown lot owner, declared Williamsburg inconvenient. Spotswood, however, took umbrage at the tone of Marable's address and declared that he was "as good a Judge as Mr. Marable's Rabble" in selecting a county seat. As a result, sometime after 1715 but before 1721, a James City County Courthouse was erected in Williamsburg, a building shared by the city and county for more than 20 years "on courtesie."

THE THREAT OF FRENCH INVASION

In 1702, after the eighteenth century superpowers England and France exchanged declarations of war, Virginia prepared in earnest for invasion. Despite its dampness and exposure to attack, the old magazine at Jamestown received a shipment of military stores. In 1706, as the French fortified their colonies in the West Indies, Virginians erected a battery platform at Jamestown designed to protect English ships as they retreated upstream. Officials believed that Jamestown Island's marshy environment made it less vulnerable to overland invasion and that "the channel of the river running so

Tower of the James City Parish Church, the only 17th century structure still standing in Jamestown. Owned by the Association for the Preservation of Virginia Antiquities. Courtesy of the National Park Service, Colonial National Historical Park.

nigh the shore" would make it impossible for enemy ships to pass by. Although the threat of a French invasion subsided for a time, by August 1711 tensions had increased again. A sloop was stationed between Capes Henry and Charles to signal the approach of enemy ships and beacons were placed at strategic sites along the colony's major rivers. If sentinels sighted enemy vessels, beacons at Jamestown and Yorktown were to be lit and two cannon shots fired. In response, all of the region's other beacons would be ignited to alert local militia units of impending invasion. New batteries at Jamestown accommodated 16 cannons protected by palisades between the James and Back rivers. Lines were laid out so that additional palisades could be erected to defend Williamsburg. William Byrd II sent 2,000 palisades for use in the defense of Jamestown and Williamsburg and a Surry County man supplied "500 pallisadoes" to Jamestown. As in the past, when the invasion threat waned, Jamestown once again neglected its fortifications and in 1725, when the gunner died, his position was abolished.

JAMESTOWN CLINGS TO LIFE

Until the mid-1700s, parishioners commuted to Jamestown to attend church. From time to time, the House of Burgesses declared public holidays, when parish churches held services throughout the colony, including Jamestown, and colonists abstained from "all Servile and bodily labour." In 1700, May 3 was appointed a day of fasting with prayers for delivery from the "great plague of caterpillars." After the "plague" subsided, a day of thanksgiving was held. August 13, 1701, and March 11, 1702, were solemnized as fast-days in anticipation of war with France and on April 23, 1702, the colonists marked the restoration of peace with a day of thanksgiving. The government sometimes planned celebrations to mark significant occasions. For example, in April 1704, Governor Francis Nicholson, despite his intense dislike of Jamestown, declared that he hoped to hold a centennial jubilee there to commemorate the colony's first settlement. But Nicholson left the colony the following year and there is no record of a centennial celebration.

Ferries traversed the James River to Swann's Point, Crouch's Creek, and Hog Island until 1779 when erosion forced construction of a new landing on the mainland. As long as these ferries docked on the island, a steady stream of visitors passed through the town. But, by 1716 when the Reverend John Fontaine visited Jamestown, he reported seeing "a small rampart with embrasures . . . deserted and gone to ruin," plus "a church, a Court House, and three or four brick houses" in disrepair. In 1747 the Reverend Hugh Jones chronicled Jamestown's continuing decline. The town, Jones wrote, consisted "of nothing but abundance of brick rubbish and three or four good inhabited houses."

Some absentee owners probably retained their lots so that they could serve as

Best Virginia Tobacco. Courtesy of the Colonial Williamsburg
Foundation.

Jamestown's delegate to the Assembly. Until 1761, a tobacco inspection warehouse existed in Jamestown, and merchant/planter Edward Jaquelin served as
the warehouse's principal inspector (and Jamestown's representative in the
Assembly). During the first half of the eighteenth century, almost all of
Jamestown Island had been absorbed into two large plantations that belonged
to wealthy and prominent families. At the western end of the island and
enveloping most of Jamestown's town lots were Edward Jaquelin's landholdings.
On the eastern end of the island and extending west along the Back River to
Kingsmill Creek and south to Passmore Creek was the plantation of the Travis
family, descendants of Ancient Planter John Johnson, one of Jamestown
Island's first patentees. Both plantations were working farms, where enslaved
African Americans labored under the watchful eye of one or more overseers or
farm managers.

THE JAQUELIN/AMBLER PLANTATION

By marriage and purchase, merchant Edward Jaquelin steadily accumulated land and influence. He immigrated to Virginia at the close of the seventeenth century and married Rachel James Sherwood, a wealthy and childless widow, who held life-rights to her previous husbands' property. Jaquelin purchased that property plus a waterfront lot in Jamestown, property on Jamestown Island, 24 acres at Glasshouse Point, and a 310-acre leasehold in the Governor's Land. He represented Jamestown in the House of Burgesses and served as a local court justice.

Although Edward Jaquelin left behind little information on how he ran his plantation, the Reverend Hugh Jones of James City Parish did describe Virginia farming practices. Local soil, Jones wrote, was well suited to the cultivation of sweet-scented tobacco (the most valuable kind). When farmers cleared forested land they cut off the trees "about a yard from the ground," hoed the earth between the stumps, and used it for planting. When the soil became exhausted by long-term cultivation of tobacco, farmers planted Indian corn, English wheat, and other crops. Wheat and corn often shared the same fields so that both crops could be harvested simultaneously. Corn was planted in hills about six feet apart and wheat was strewn upon the ground and then trod with the hooves of horses.

Racial Tensions

In 1705, the House of Burgesses inserted racism into Virginia's legal code. They officially relegated enslaved African Americans to the status of personal property that could be bought and sold. Indians lost legal rights previously guaranteed, precisely at a time when the tributary Indians were making increased use of the colony's judicial system. Under the 1705 legal code, Indians and other non-whites could no longer testify in court, a restriction that prevented them from collecting debts. Indian bondservants could not sue for freedom if their masters detained them after their contract expired. Inter-racial marriage became illegal, and non-whites became ineligible for all public offices.

In March 1710, several Jamestown slaves were implicated in a failed rebellion that involved African Americans and Indians in Surry and Isle of Wight counties. One of the accused belonged to Edward Jaquelin, then the local sheriff. Others lived in the households of the Reverend James Blair (rector of James City Parish), Edward Ross (ferryman and gunner of Jamestown's fort), Philip Ludwell, George Marable, and John Brodnax. Most of the slaves were released into the custody of their owners "to receive correction," but Essex (who belonged to Ross) and Jamy (who was owned by Brodnax) were executed as an example to others.

A 1711 law required both tributary and non-tributary Indians to wear badges when they entered colonized areas, and in 1714 a law prohibited the use of the titles "king" and "queen" in reference to native leaders. Thus, as Virginia's Indians became increasingly acculturated and assumed a more visible (but less forceful) role in society, they became legally susceptible to the same types of discrimination endured by African Americans.

Ruins of Ambler House, a Georgian mansion that stood from circa 1754 to 1895. Courtesy of the National Park Service, Colonial National Historical Park.

As most Virginians allowed their hogs to forage for roots in the marshes and woods, Edward Jaquelin's plantation, which included much of Pitch and Tar Swamp, was ideally suited to raising swine. The Reverend Jones said that the quality of Virginia beef and veal was excellent but that its pork was famous, especially bacon and hams. In the Tidewater, wild fowl, fish (including sheepshead, rock, trout, drum, and sturgeon), and shellfish (oysters and crabs) were plentiful, but venison was not then as abundant as it had been. Mulberry trees and fruit trees grew well, and many Virginians made cider from their apples, which they drank liberally. Planters also made a beverage from persimmons and produced beer from molasses or raised barley and made malt. The most common imported malt-drink was Bristol beer, which Virginians consumed in large quantities the year around. Madeira, Virginia's most popular wine, reputedly relieved the heat of summer and warmed "the chilled blood in the bitter colds of winter." Affluent Virginians, like Edward Jaquelin and the Travises, consumed European wine, especially claret and port, and enjoyed chocolate, coffee, and tea. Virginia farmers, according to Reverend Jones, led relatively easy lives and let their slaves do much of their

Sketch of the wheat machine that Ebinezer Hazard saw behind the Ambler mansion in 1777.
Courtesy of the Colonial Williamsburg Foundation.

work. They spent much of their time riding or racing horses, playing cards, and visiting friends.

In 1734 some of the town's lot owners asked the House of Burgesses for funds to stabilize the riverbanks at Sandy Bay, where the James and Back Rivers met. They contended that recently the "great breaches between the river and creek at Sandy Bay" made it dangerous to cross over to Jamestown Island. Their request was denied. Two years later, the petitioners informed the burgesses that the causeway leading to the public ferry on Jamestown Island was so badly eroded that the tide sometimes inundated it. But again, their request for funds was denied. In 1748 "several responsible freeholders" offered to keep the road in good repair if the ferry landing were moved to their lots in Jamestown. They asked that Richard Ambler (who by then owned the Jaquelin property) be required to repair the causeway or lose his right to operate the ferry. Ambler, a burgess, protested and the ferry stayed where it was. Around 1750, when a new parish church was built on the mainland, the road probably became less of an aggravation, for people did not have to use it when making their obligatory weekly commute to worship services.

Richard Ambler, who immigrated to Virginia in 1716 at age 26, settled in Yorktown, where he became a prosperous merchant. In 1729, he married Edward Jaquelin's eldest daughter, Elizabeth. Jaquelin, who died in November 1739, bequeathed life-rights to his Jamestown Island landholdings to his son-in-law and gave him a waterfront lot near the ferry landing at Orchard Run.

Ambler's next of kin described him as just under six feet tall and plump. His ability to accumulate wealth bears mute testimony to his business acumen. He quickly consolidated more than a dozen Jamestown Island parcels into a substantial plantation that he developed into a family seat. In January 1745 he purchased nearly 300 acres from Christopher Perkins and obtained an unencumbered title to his late father-in-law's land in April. Richard Ambler's consolidation of the Perkins and Jaquelin landholdings enabled him to amass nearly 700 acres in the southern and western portions of Jamestown Island, enveloping almost all of its James River shoreline. At mid-century Ambler built an imposing brick dwelling in the heart of New Towne but continued to live in Yorktown.

When Ambler died in February 1766, he left his Jamestown Island plantation and its Georgian mansion to his eldest son, John Ambler I, who already resided there. He also gave John his leasehold on the mainland, some acreage at nearby Powhatan Plantation, and all of the household furnishings, agricultural equipment, slaves, and livestock associated with all of his James City County property. An inventory counted a total of 77 slaves. John Ambler I, an attorney educated in England, represented Jamestown in the House of Burgesses from 1759 to 1765 and served as Collector of Customs for the York District. He died on May 27, 1766, outliving his father by only three months. John Ambler I's landholdings descended to his brother, Edward. Edward, who had inherited Richard Ambler's home in Yorktown, moved into the brick mansion on Jamestown Island. He succeeded his brother in the House of Burgesses. But Edward, "after a tedious illness," died on October 30, 1768, leaving a widow and six-year-old son. Two months later, tragedy struck again. In late December one of the Ambler plantation outbuildings at Jamestown burned to the ground and "a valuable Negro man, attempting to save some of his effects, perished in the flames."

The widowed Mary Cary Ambler, who revered Jamestown for its antiquity, continued to live there. She withdrew only when Jamestown Island became a combat zone during the Revolutionary War. At Mrs. Ambler's death, an immense estate descended to their son, John Ambler II, who came of age in 1783. He inherited the ancestral plantation on Jamestown Island, his grandfather's leasehold on the mainland, part of Powhatan Plantation, and thousands of acres in several other counties.

THE TRAVIS PLANTATION

Edward Champion Travis, whose great-grandfather came into possession of his land on the eastern end of Jamestown Island through marriage to Ancient Planter John Johnson's daughter, inherited his forebears' approximately 840-acre plantation. Travis, who was one of the area's most affluent citizens, served as a burgess and colonel in the local militia. He had an interest in the slave trade and during the 1750s his sloop, the James Town, carried small numbers of Africans from Barbados to Virginia. During the early 1770s, Travis moved to a plantation in York County leaving his son, Champion, to live in the family home on Jamestown Island. Champion, like his father, took an active role in public life. He represented Jamestown in the House of Burgesses, participated in the Conventions of 1774 and 1775, held the rank of colonel in a district battalion, and served as a county justice and sheriff. He was appointed a naval commissioner in 1776. The old Travis home remained in Champion's hands until after the American Revolution. In December 1778 Champion left his Jamestown Island plantation to his son.

Chapter 7

JAMESTOWN ISLAND AND THE
REVOLUTIONARY WAR

By late summer 1775 the breach between Great Britain and her American colonies had become irreparable. Because Jamestown Island's proximity to the James River channel gave it strategic importance, the Ambler and Travis plantations stood in the midst of combat throughout much of the war. On November 1 British boats headed upriver and exchanged shots with Americans when they passed Jamestown. A few cannonballs hit the ferry house. Subsequently the schooner *Kingsfisher* sailed upriver, joined by two sloops. Unable to destroy Burwell's Ferry, they reached Jamestown on the 14th accompanied by a reinforcing tender. That night the British sent a ship's boat to Jamestown, but it was detected by American sentinels and driven off. The larger boats fired on Jamestown as well, but one ran aground on a sandbar, and soldiers on the Surry side of the river joined the fracas. In this phase of fighting a British shell perforated the Travis' kitchen chimney. The Americans seized the sloop, outfitted it for use by Virginia's state navy, and placed it under the command of Captain Edward Travis, whose brother Champion lived on Jamestown Island. In 1776 Champion Travis informed the Virginia Convention that "his dwelling-house and offices thereunto belonging in the town of Jamestown for many months past have been and are now occupied and appropriated by a detachment from the Virginia army as guardhouses."

During this period Lord Dunmore's men, despite the Virginians' resistance, cruised Tidewater's navigable waterways, landing almost anywhere at will. Dunmore declared martial law in Virginia and signed an Emancipation Proclamation, freeing all slaves and indentured servants and encouraging them to bear arms on behalf of the king. Two slaves who offered their services to the

Virginia Militiaman, 1780. Painting by Don Troiani, www.historicalartprints.com

crew of what they assumed was a British ship were executed at Jamestown by the Americans they mistakenly approached.

THE STRUGGLE FOR INDEPENDENCE

In May 1776, when British General Henry Clinton invaded North Carolina, Virginia troops marched to oppose him. This gave rise to fears about Williamsburg's vulnerability. Delegates to the Fifth Virginia Convention decided to station a strong force in Williamsburg, Jamestown, Yorktown, Hampton, and at Burwell's Ferry. During the spring and summer two militia companies camped at Burwell's Ferry, where they constructed fortifications and worked on the road to Williamsburg. At Jamestown, a battalion of minutemen under Colonel Charles Lewis, despite ill health, built a curvilinear battery that stood in a low-lying area west of the old church, near the site occupied by a brick battery a century earlier.

Throughout 1776 Jamestown Island bustled with military activity. Baggage, ammunition, heavy weapons, flour, tools, salt, tobacco, and various commodities arrived to be loaded aboard outbound vessels. Scottish Highlanders, captured en route to Lord Dunmore, were brought ashore at Jamestown. Captain Edward Travis used Jamestown Island to outfit and repair the naval vessels under his command.

When high tide stranded Ebenezer Hazard on Jamestown Island in June 1777, he went exploring and left a wartime description of Jamestown. Hazard depicted Jamestown as gloomy. He noted that "a little above the town" stood a small battery garrisoned by a dozen or so Allied soldiers. He visited the graveyard of the old, abandoned church and transcribed William Sherwood's epitaph, "A Great Sinner Waiting For A Joyfull Resurrection." Hazard found a fine but badly neglected fruit orchard at Jamestown and Mrs. Ambler's abandoned home, now in use as a ferry house. "Delightfully situated," the rapidly decaying brick house had large, well papered rooms with "lofty Ceilings, Marble Hearths and other Indications of Elegance and Taste." Hazard closed by saying that "the other houses in town are wooden and all in ruins."

A German visitor, George Daniel Flohr, also commented that what once "was a large city" was "completely ruined now." Dr. James Thatcher, an American contemporary with a sense of history, wrote that "the most ancient settlement in America . . . cannot now be called a town, there being but two houses standing on the banks of the river."

THE TRAVIS AND AMBLER PLANTATIONS

When Mrs. Mary Ambler fled Jamestown Island she moved to her late husband's Hanover County plantation, where she resided until her death. Fortunately, she took a collection of manuscripts accumulated by her husband's family documenting their land titles throughout Virginia. These papers provide invaluable insights into land ownership patterns on Jamestown Island.

Mrs. Mary Ambler leased to Captain Edward Travis "all buildings and other appurtenances and advantages" on her property at Jamestown "except a Nursery adjoining the Mansion House which is to be reserved for the use of the ferry." This four-year lease briefly gave the Travises, Edward and Champion, possession of Jamestown Island in its entirety, with the possible exception of a few town lots. The agreement became effective on January 13, 1780. Captain Travis subdivided Mrs. Ambler's arable land into three parts, placing only one under cultivation at a time. Under the terms of the lease, Travis was prohibited from converting forested land into open fields or from cutting timber other than firewood. Mrs. Ambler reserved the right to leave her livestock upon the island and to gather hay and fruit.

Shortly before Mrs. Ambler leased her plantation, a group of local citizens successfully asked the state assembly to move the ferry landing from Jamestown Island to the mainland. They cited the prohibitive cost of maintaining the causeway recently breached by tidal waters.

THE CAPITAL RELOCATES AGAIN

On June 12, 1779, the General Assembly voted to move Virginia's capital from Williamsburg to Richmond, a centralized location presumed safer from enemy attack. On April 7, 1780, the state's executive department ceased transacting business in Williamsburg and on the 24th it resumed its duties in Richmond. During the first week of May, the Assembly held its first session in the new capital. Afterward, Williamsburg declined, mirroring Jamestown's demise in 1699.

THE BRITISH MILITARY BUILD-UP

In mid-April 1781 British General William Phillips arrived in Hampton Roads with an army 2,600 strong. On the 21st, American Colonel James Innes informed the governor that the British had landed at Burwell's Landing and that 500 infantrymen were marching toward Williamsburg, forcing Innes to withdraw hastily in the middle of the night. As he composed his message to the governor, Innes received word that 14 enemy ships had sailed above Jamestown and that their flat-bottomed boats were ascending the Chickahominy River. Meanwhile, General Phillips and a large body of troops marched to Barretts Ferry, at the

British Forty-Third Regiment of Foot. Courtesy of The Anne S. K. Brown Military Collection, Brown University Library.

mouth of the Chickahominy, and boarded naval vessels that transported them to the mouth of the Appomattox River. These events set the stage for what happened at Jamestown a few months later.

In late May Charles Lord Cornwallis and his army of seasoned veterans arrived in Petersburg, where they joined forces with Phillips' men, temporarily under the command of General Benedict Arnold. This union of forces created a British Army numbering 7,000. Cornwallis crossed the James River and set out in pursuit of the Marquis de Lafayette, who had retreated toward Fredericksburg while awaiting reinforcements. The young French general embarked upon a strategy of paralleling the British Army's movements, staying just out of reach.

THE BATTLE OF GREEN SPRING

As both armies parried each other's movements, the British occupied Williamsburg and destroyed some horseboats they found on Jamestown Island. On

June 30, 1781, Cornwallis notified his superiors that he intended to move to Jamestown so that his men could cross the James River. On July 4 the main body of the British Army, encamped on the Ambler farm on the mainland, prepared to evacuate. Meanwhile, Lafayette moved his advance units east to a point approximately ten miles above Williamsburg. Thinking that the main body of the British Army already had crossed the James, he decided to move closer to Jamestown and attack whatever enemy troops remained. He dispatched a detachment of men under General Anthony Wayne to Jamestown, but held the greater part of his force in reserve.

Lafayette had fallen prey to false intelligence. The British had paid two local men to tell any American troops they saw that the British had left the area. As luck would have it, one of the men encountered General Wayne, to whom he imparted the misinformation.

French Gatinois Regiment of Infantry.
Courtesy of The Anne S.K. Brown Military
Collection, Brown University Library.

Early in the afternoon of July 6, Wayne and the Pennsylvania Line reached Green Spring plantation. There he paused and decided to test the strength of his enemy. Around 2 P. M. a small group of

The Marquis de Lafayette, 1779. Painting by Charles Wilson Peale. Courtesy of the Washington-Custis-Lee Collection, Washington and Lee University, Lexington, Virginia.

Anthony Wayne by Sharples. Courtesy of Independence National Historical Park.

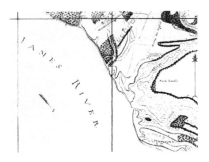

Detail of Plan du terrain a la Rive Gauche de la Riviere de James by Jean-Nicolas Desandrouin, 1781. Courtesy of the Library of Congress.

American riflemen and a scouting party advanced across the long, narrow causeway that extended toward Jamestown. They exchanged fire with a British cavalry patrol and then with British pickets, who fired and fell back. Slowly, the Americans entered Cornwallis's carefully contrived trap. When Lafayette arrived at Green Spring, he still assumed that the British were continuing to withdraw across the James. Only when he moved to a vantage point on the river bank did he realize that he had been duped and that the British remained in force. Hurrying back to Green Spring Lafayette ordered two battalions of Virginia troops to an open field at the causeway's western end where they could cover General Wayne's inevitable retreat.

Meanwhile, Wayne's men, still unaware of the ruse, continued toward Jamestown. Following a British field piece that was slowly being withdrawn, they suddenly came face to face with enemy troops concealed in the woods. Wayne realized that he had entered a trap, launched a momentary attack to check the British and avert panic among his men, and then withdrew to the narrow causeway and fled under cover of the firepower provided by the Virginians. As darkness fell both sides retired from the battlefield, and Lafayette moved further inland, leaving three companies of light infantry at Green Spring. At daybreak on July 7 British Lieutenant Colonel Banastre Tarleton, with 200 dragoons and 80 mounted infantrymen, crossed the Green Spring causeway. When he encountered a patrol of mounted American riflemen, both sides withdrew. That night the British departed from Jamestown Island and Lafayette took up a position on the mainland, where his enemies had encamped only two days before.

A soldier, who returned to the battlefield after all fighting had ceased, reported that both armies' lines could be traced by trails of empty cartridge boxes on the ground. In September 1781 an American officer informed his superiors that he had "employed a person to collect from the people the arms picked up after the action at Jamestown, which are chiefly State property." As late as the mid-nineteenth century traces of the Battle of Green Spring were still visible. Historian Benson J. Lossing, who visited the owner of the Ambler farm on the mainland at that time, said that the dwelling had "many bullet marks, made there during the battle at Jamestown Ford, on the 6th of July, 1781."

JAMESTOWN AT THE CLOSE OF THE WAR

An agreement negotiated during spring 1781 provided for exchanges of prisoners-of-war at Jamestown. When the newly released American detainees arrived they were in desperate need of provisions, medical attention, money, and transportation, but they found widespread destruction. The Chevalier d'Ancteville, who arrived at Jamestown in late summer 1781, wrote of "burned debris, tombs opened, other beautiful monuments broken to pieces, a temple partly knocked down." He claimed that "the houses still existing breathed a cadaverous odor and enclosed cadavers." "All means of devastation," he wrote, "had been employed to the city and to the countryside."

In September 1781, when the Allied Army arrived at Jamestown and made preparations to cross the James, the Marquis de St. Simone inspected the island. He ordered his men to encamp near the isthmus, which at low tide provided access to the mainland. St. Simone noted that "the bridge of Cornwallis had been destroyed," implying that the British had erected some sort of span that linked the island with the mainland. When the Allies left Jamestown on September 4, they waded through waist-deep water and hand-carried their artillery.

Later, French troops streamed into the area as part of the overall military build-up that preceded the siege of Yorktown. The troops of Jean-Francois-Louis, Comte de Clermont-Crevecour, who had sailed from Annapolis on September 20 and arrived at Jamestown five days later, disembarked near the mouth of College Creek, and set out for Williamsburg as soon as their weapons and supplies came ashore. Contemporary maps reveal that large numbers of French troops camped on the eastern end of Jamestown Island and that buildings were scattered throughout what had been urban Jamestown, structures most probably associated with the Ambler plantation and the Travis's town home.

❖

View Of Jamestown. Painting by Louis Girardin, 1805. Courtesy of the Colonial Williamsburg Foundation.

Chapter 8

THE FLOWERING OF
A NEW NATION

RECOVERY FROM THE WAR

After the French and British went home, the people of eastern Virginia began
to rebuild their lives. Financial problems plagued many local families during the
postwar period, even though taxes were payable in commodities such as wheat,
rye, oats, barley, corn, and bacon. In 1785 the county sheriff asked the state legislature to dismiss the charges against him for delinquency in collecting local
taxes. He cited "the hardships of the people due to shortness of crops during the
past year as a reason for their not being able to pay taxes promptly." An identi-
cal request was put forth the following year because local citizens "were exceed-
ingly poor and unable to pay taxes."

Some suffered severe economic hardships. Jamestown ferry-keeper Dionysius
Lester sought payment for transporting American soldiers across the James, and
a Surry County woman requested compensation for a slave captured by Lord
Dunmore's forces while ferrying Virginia troops. Champion Travis sought compensation from the government for his Jamestown dwelling and offices ruined
when Virginia troops used them as guardhouses. Tax records suggest that during the late 1780s and early 1790s Champion Travis's fortunes waned. It is
probable that he, like many other staunch supporters of the American cause,
went deeply into debt during the war. The number of slaves and the amount of
livestock that he owned decreased markedly. Travis's crops and farm animals,
like those of the Amblers, undoubtedly fell prey to foraging armies, and some
of his slaves may have fled to the British who offered them freedom. William
Lee of Green Spring claimed that "a Dutch blanket wrapt round the shoulders
and fasten before with a skewer is now . . . the most common form of great

Coat." John Ambler II and other leaseholders of the Governor's Land refused to pay taxes on the acreage they rented.

THE AMBLER PLANTATION

Not everyone suffered equally. Edward and Mary Ambler's son, John Ambler II, who came of age in 1783 and inherited the family plantation on Jamestown Island, was one of Tidewater Virginia's wealthiest farmers. His household accounts reveal that he procured much of his family's clothing, footwear, and furniture from London, but relied heavily on local merchants for everyday items. A Richmond tailor sometimes fashioned the family's clothing but Williamsburg goldsmith James Galt repaired and cleaned John Ambler II's watches and mended his incense case. Ambler had his blacksmithing done at Green Spring and hired local craftsmen to repair his saddle and farming equipment and make a wheat machine. He paid local practitioners for dentistry and for inoculating household members against smallpox. Wheat and pork were sold locally, usually in large quantities.

As proprietor of much of Jamestown, John Ambler II enclosed the church's graveyard with a brick wall. He also built a log-and-stone causeway at the mouth of Sandy Bay that reconnected Jamestown Island with the mainland. Nonetheless, in October 1798 when four local men visited the Amblers at Jamestown, they found the causeway inundated by the tide. According to Williamsburg's Dr. Philip Barraud, the portly Bishop James Madison climbed out of the coach and insisted on crossing on foot. But before he had gone far, he toppled into the river and had to be rescued. After a good meal at John Ambler's and an ample supply of wine, one of the Bishop's companions waggishly observed that "his Holiness received this correction as a Lesson not to assume so broad a Bottom for the Mother Church" and reminded him that, notwithstanding his piety, he was unable to walk on water.

Despite Ambler's economic prowess, his life was far from idyllic. His first and second wives "fell martyrs to their attachment to Jamestown . . . known to be unhealthy during the months of August and September." In 1799, when he married for the third time, Ambler resolved to spend only the winter months there. He placed his Jamestown Island plantation, slaves, and livestock in the hands of overseer Henry Taylor, whom he paid in crop-shares.

Even though the Ambler plantation covered almost all of Jamestown Island's western end, during the late eighteenth century a few town lots belonged to others. In 1771 William and Hannah Philippa Ludwell Lee came into possession of two Jamestown lots, one with a building previously owned by the late Philip Ludwell III. John Parke Custis, who inherited two or more Jamestown lots that he considered of little or no value, in May 1778 asked his step-father, George Washington, if he should sell them. In time the Lee and Custis lots became part of the Ambler family's holdings.

During the early nineteenth century John Ambler II and his family lived in Richmond most of the year. His son Edward Ambler II moved to Jamestown around 1809 and made it his home. Six years later his father gave him the property, along with its slaves and livestock. In 1820, when Virginia's tax assessors began listing the value of the buildings and land, Edward Ambler II's 900-acre Jamestown Island plantation had structures worth $3,600, making it one of the area's most valuable farms. Ambler sold his property in 1821 and it changed hands twice more within the year. Finally, in 1822, David Bullock of Richmond purchased the Ambler farm and, in 1831, he acquired the Travis plantation. These transactions gave him possession of Jamestown Island in its entirety, property he retained through 1835.

THE TRAVIS PLANTATION

In 1782 Champion Travis, who inherited nearly 800 acres at the eastern end of Jamestown Island, had a substantial number of slaves and a large livestock herd. Like other wealthy planters who owned several tracts of land, he entrusted his plantation to the care of an overseer. In May 1793 two slaves, Nelly and Daphney, who were plowing Travis's fields on Jamestown Island, attacked and killed overseer Joel Gathright. According to official accounts, Gathright had berated the women for allowing sheep to get into a cornfield and then struck one of them. As the beating continued, the women fought back. One picked up a stone and dealt the overseer a mortal blow. Both slaves were tried, found guilty of murder, and sentenced to hang. Although some neighboring landowners asked the governor to spare the life of one slave who was pregnant, another group urged him to execute her as an example to others. The latter view prevailed.

Champion Travis's Jamestown Island plantation descended to his son, Samuel, in 1818. When the tax assessor visited the property in 1820, it had no taxable improvements.

A NEED FOR MILITARY DEFENSE

Even after the close of the Revolutionary War, local militia units continued to drill regularly in their home communities. In a holdover from the colonial era, the militia elected their own officers, although the governor actually issued military commissions. Most of the men chosen served as county justices or held other important government positions. Thus, even after the Revolution, the families that traditionally monopolized political power remained highly influential. In 1787 Lieutenant Colonel Champion Travis held one of the highest ranks in James City County's militia, and in 1797, Captain John Ambler II of Jamestown Island commanded the local cavalry.

THE WAR OF 1812 AND ITS AFTERMATH

During James Madison's second term as president, hostilities between Great Britain and France ensnared the United States. Shortly after war broke out, Governor James Barbour visited Jamestown. Once again the strategic value of the island became apparent. Although the governor concluded that Jamestown was a good site for a fort, no action was taken to secure the position. Months later the British blockaded Hampton Roads and in early February 1813, local infantrymen were sent to Norfolk and Hampton to repel a potential invasion. This, in essence, left the peninsula defenseless. On June 25, 1813, 900 British troops marched toward Williamsburg while ships in the James River fired on people on shore. Despite the regiment that reinforced Williamsburg from two

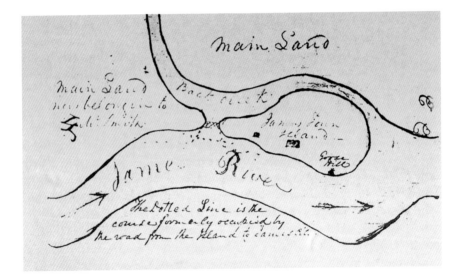

Sketch map showing a toll bridge built at Jamestown Island in 1832. Courtesy of the James City County Clerk of Court and the Library of Virginia.

nearby counties, 14 British barges, an armed brig, and six or seven tenders moved freely up and down the James River, plundering waterfront homes and sometimes venturing inland. Colonel John Ambler II was stationed at Camp Bottoms Bridge on July 1, 1813, when the British invaded his home on Jamestown Island. The raiding party, "after plundering the plantation, destroyed...furniture of every description." The British reportedly carried off whatever they could and laid waste to the rest. On July 5 a British brig, several schooners and eight or ten barges passed by Jamestown Island and continued upstream. In April 1814 a high-ranking military officer recommended that a fort and battery be built at Jamestown or further up the James to prevent the British from reaching Richmond. Again, no action was taken.

After hostilities ceased, Virginia entered a period of economic stagnation and America experienced its first great depression, the Panic of 1819. Agricultural prices plummeted. Most of the farmland east of the Blue Ridge was exhausted by generations of use without replenishment. Land prices dropped and many Tidewater families moved west.

But when farmers learned that lime and marl would restore the fertility of soil acidified by the long-term production of tobacco, local economic conditions began to improve. By the early 1840s land values in the Tidewater had improved significantly and farm income had increased.

A BRIDGE TO JAMESTOWN ISLAND

In 1832 two local entrepreneurs, Goodrich Durfey and William Edloe, asked the General Assembly to move the James River ferry landing back to Jamestown Island, where steamboats and ferries could dock more conveniently. The two men wanted to erect a toll bridge across the Back River and link the island with the mainland. But John Hill Smith, then-owner of the mainland Ambler farm and ferry landing, strenuously objected. He contended that "the old road on the Jamestown side has been wholly washed away by the river and the place where it ran is now in the river at a distance of 75 or 100 yards from the present shore." He added that "on the opposite side of the creek [where his farm was located] the former road is partly covered by water" and had been abandoned for more than 50 years. He also pointed out that his late father-in-law, John Ambler II, had built "a stone bridge [causeway] across the creek at a great distance from the old road, which was good as long as it lasted."

The General Assembly, over Smith's protests, moved the ferry landing to Jamestown Island and approved the bridge proposal. The new span, which was in place by January 1833, stood near the site where John Ambler II had built a causeway.

JAMESTOWN ISLAND AS A WORKING FARM

David Bullock of Richmond, who in 1831 came into possession of Jamestown Island in its entirety, sold it to bridge concessionaire Goodrich Durfey in 1835. Within a decade Durfey, a real estate speculator, offered it for sale. He claimed that nearly half of the 2,000-acre farm had been marled and limed and was "in a high state of improvement and cultivation." The island was described as having "the best wheat soil in the state" and ample pasturage for 300 head of cattle. According to Durfey's 1844 newspaper advertisement, there was "a substantial three story brick house, 40 by 60, with 4 rooms on a floor, in good repair" and "a kitchen, a laundry, an overseer's house, a dairy, a smokehouse, barns and stables, together with negro houses, all of which are new and in good order." The farm also had "a young apple and peach orchard of the best improved fruit from Baltimore and Richmond nurseries" and a ferry and steamboat wharf that produced $300 a year apiece.

In 1845 Durfey sold Jamestown Island to John Coke, then-owner of the old Ambler farm on the mainland. Coke moved to the island, but in 1847 he sold it to Martha Orgain, whose young son, William, was the nephew and principal heir of William Allen of Claremont. When young William came of age and assumed his uncle's surname (a prerequisite to receiving his inheritance), he assumed control of Jamestown Island, more than 3,000 acres in the Neck O'Land behind the island, and the Kingsmill and Littletown plantations. Thus, his river frontage extended from the western end of Jamestown Island east to Grove Creek. Allen, like his late uncle, resided at Claremont, entrusting his outlying properties to a principal overseer who supervised local farm managers. Large herds of livestock were pastured on Jamestown Island while cultivated fields produced abundant crops of corn and grain. Meanwhile, across Sandy Bay on the mainland, John Coke and his wife retained the farm called "Amblers."

SOJOURNS AT JAMESTOWN

Throughout the nineteenth century Jamestown attracted considerable attention from history-conscious travelers, including several who prepared written accounts of what they observed.

In May 1807, while John Ambler II was still in possession of the ancestral plantation at Jamestown, a centenary celebration commemorated the first colonists' arrival. Although relatively little is known about the "immense assembly which was convened on the plains of Jamestown," it is certain that a number of distinguished citizens and some students from the College of William and Mary delivered orations. One eyewitness said that "Many yards of the palisades erected by the first settlers are yet to be seen at a low tide standing at least 150 to 200 paces [375 to 500 feet] from the present shore." The posts he saw probably were remnants of the approximately 2,000 palisades used to fortify Jamestown Island in 1711 against an expected French invasion.

John Henry Strobia, who visited Jamestown Island in July 1817, noted that "few traces of its ancient importance" were in evidence. "Two or three old houses, the ruins of an old steeple, a church yard and faint marks of rude fortifications are now the only memorials of its former inhabitants." English diarist Henry Beaumont, who tarried at Jamestown in 1818, commented on "an old house built of brick," part of which had fallen down. He said that the dwelling "appeared as if it had a long time been abandoned and was all overgrown with weeds and wild berries." Accompanied by a fellow traveler, the pair agreed that "old James Town" was "a fine situation for a Town" and discussed the merits of purchasing and developing the island. But when they learned that it would be difficult to obtain a clear title to the property, they promptly discarded the idea.

In 1822, the year David Bullock bought the Ambler plantation, a celebration commemorated the first colonists' arrival. Thousands of visitors flocked to the island. One man said that the celebrants, in their unbridled enthusiasm, "burnt down one of the two large brick houses on the island [the Travis house] and broke the tombstones into fragments and scattered them over the face of the earth so that the whole island exhibited one wide field of desolation." A journalist reported that five steamboats, 35 other vessels, and an infinite number of small boats brought even more tourists to Jamestown Island than had attended the 1807 celebration. There were no formal ceremonies or speeches, and throngs of visitors dispersed to go picnicking.

In 1837, while Goodrich Durfey owned Jamestown Island, historian Charles Campbell stopped by. He wrote that "all that remains of Jamestown" was "the fragment of a wall of the old church, standing solitary in a ploughed field." The water "is gaining on the land and the time may not be far off when the ground on which it stood shall be submerged." Richard Randolph, who also visited the island in 1837, spoke of seeing the church ruins, "some of the remains of the walls and mounds of the ancient fortress of Jamestown," and "a small brick building that tradition says was a powder magazine." He added that

> . . . at a little distance from this house are the remains . . . of a very large building. This was apparently the Governor's or State House. There are similar remains in other places lying on the surface of the ground in regular order in a long, narrow line, which probably indicates the direction and location of the principal streets of the town.

And, "in digging the foundation of a house in the Island some time since the workmen discovered several human skeletons. Indeed, these may be found in many places near the site of the town."

Although Randolph believed that the oldest part of Jamestown lay west of the fort ruins, he said that:

> The part of the Island not embraced within the limits of a town appears to have been apportioned into numerous lots of small size, each one of which was surrounded by a dyke. Many of these ditches are still visible and plainly indicate the extent of the lots they enclosed. On some of these lots are to be found remains of buildings. On one there is an old well, the brick walls of which are quite perfect and sound.

When Randolph returned to Jamestown at mid-century, he mistakenly concluded that

> . . . the great body of the town, which however was never very large, was certainly west of the Old Steeple [or church tower] still visible, and is

Distant View Of Jamestown Island, 1850-1851. Sketched by Benson Lossing. Courtesy of the Colonial Williamsburg Foundation.

now entirely or very nearly submerged in the river. This is clearly proved by the old deeds for lots in the town, recorded in the office of James City County court, which call for bounds that are now under water; and more palpably, by vast numbers of broken bricks, and other relics of buildings that may still be seen in the Western bank at low tide.

Mansfield Lovell, who toured the peninsula in 1843, said that Jamestown then had a brick house, two frame buildings, and the ruins of an old church belfry. When Benjamin J. Lossing visited the island a few years later, he stayed with its owner, John Coke, who had "all the soil that is left unsubmerged on which the English built their first town in America." Lossing paused on the western bank of Sandy Bay and made a sketch of distant Jamestown Island, noting that "what was once a marsh" had become "a deep bay, 400 yards wide." He drew "the remains of a bridge, destroyed by a gale and high tide a few years ago," and said that his host was living upon the island when the storm occurred. According to Coke, the storm inundated the island and "for three days himself and his family were prisoners." He reportedly "was obliged to cut the branches of ornamental trees close to his house" to obtain fuel. Coke said that his father-in-law "well remembered when a marsh, so narrow and firm that a person might cross it upon a fence rail, was where the deep water at the ruined bridge now is." Lossing, like others before him, predicted that within a few years Jamestown Island would "have a navigable channel around it, so great was the encroach-

Site Of The Old Colonial Fort. Painitng by Robert Sully in 1854. Courtesy of the National Park Service, Colonial National Historical Park.

ment of the waters of the river." He added that "already a large portion of it, whereon the ancient town was erected, has been washed away," and that "a cypress-tree, now many yards from the shore, stood at the end of a carriage-way to the wharf, 60 yards from the water's edge, only 16 years ago." Lossing urged Virginians to build a masonry wall to check the river's encroachment and closed by saying that "some remains of the old fort may be seen at low water several yards from the shore."

Historian Henry Howe also visited Jamestown Island during the mid-nineteenth century and recorded his observations. He said that the first fort had stood upon "a point of land projecting into the James" and added that "the water is gaining on the shore, and the time will arrive when the waves will roll over it." President Millard Filmore, who traveled to Richmond by steamer during the early 1850s, paused at Jamestown to savor its antiquity and explore the old cemetery and church ruins.

One of the most eloquent visitors to Jamestown Island was artist Robert Sully, who chronicled his 1854 sojourn and illustrated it with pencil sketches and watercolor paintings. He produced pictures of the church tower, the Travis house ruins, and a cypress tree he estimated stood 60 yards off shore. He also sketched "the site of the old fort," which he said was "two hundred yards above the church, on an elevated point." Sully indicated that the foundation of a magazine, "still in good preservation" and made "of the same kind of bricks as the church," stood 40 yards behind the fort site and had a 10 foot square powder pit that extended to a depth of "about 5 feet." William Allen's overseer, who was Sully's host, gave him an old musket barrel he had recovered from the fort point and admitted to having "some blue beads, Indian arrow heads, a stone hatchet, Indian pipe bowls, &c."

Sully noted that "the encroachment of the water on the land has been long going on, but of late years, particularly at the point where the Church stands, it has been fearfully rapid." Just "a little below the Fort Point, there is some distance from the beach a Cypress Tree, under water to its lower branches" and that "in the recollection of the living, Carriages once drove around this tree." Moreover, "a considerable distance from the Beach, at low water, there is distinctly seen the Inclosure of a well Brick'd round in a circle." Sully observed that "at a former period, the little tongue of land on which the Church stands projected much further out - a gentle slope. It is now washed away to an abrupt half circle."

THE 1857 CELEBRATION

In 1854 the Jamestown Society of Washington began planning a celebration to commemorate the 250th anniversary of the first settlers' arrival. Members joined with the Virginia Historical Society and, with the full cooperation of the island's owner William Allen, began erecting cabins to accommodate visitors. They also built a 175-foot-long refreshment saloon, a dining hall that seated 500, and a speaker's platform. As May 13 drew near, celebrants from Washington, Baltimore, Norfolk, and Richmond boarded steamboats destined for the Jamestown Celebration. Soon "a large fleet of bright winged craft of all sizes and characters, jubilant with gay streamers, booming guns and sonorous music" floated off Jamestown Island. By noon 13 steamers, several schooners, and a yacht had congregated. Several bands filled the air with music.

One visitor noted that "all that remains at Jamestown is a portion of the tower and walls of the old church and a brick magazine, now used as a barn." Another said that souvenir-hunters "cracked off a suitable chunk from one of the old slabs" in the graveyard, while others "contented themselves with a brickbat apiece" from the old church tower. According to a news account "a beautiful grove and wild thicket of underbrush" then surrounded the church ruins. "Beyond the grove, on all sides, the land is cleared and under high cultivation; about two hundred acres nearest the church are in wheat." The Jamestown Celebration included patriotic rhetoric, an elaborate military review, dancing, and free-flowing champagne. The day was hot and Judge John B. Clopton's son, William, told a friend that his elderly father was exhausted by the "hard walking through corn fields" and kept insisting, "Take me to the stand," which the younger man interpreted to mean the speaker's stand. But when they neared the podium the judge declared, "I don't want to hear John Tyler now. Take me to the stand where the mint julep is!"

Three illustrations by David H. Strother ("Porte Crayon"), published in *Harper's Weekly* in 1857, depict the church ruins at Jamestown, the celebration's military encampment, and a prone celebrant on the waterfront imbibing from a jug. Strother wrote that:

> Drums were beating, colors flying, pots boiling and glasses rattling; gallant-looking officers on horseback were galloping about the field; companies of soldiers were marching and maneuvering, while the great unorganized mass just swarmed about the pavilions, without doing anything in particular that we could perceive.

He added that "the field was alive with tents; among them a huge one, in which every variety of gambling was in full blast" until the commanding officer found out. The 1857 celebration ended with "everybody pleased, everybody tired, and almost everybody sober." Although many of the merrymakers departed from Jamestown Island, those who stayed overnight were treated to fireworks and a grand ball.

Mid-nineteenth century issues of the *Virginia Gazette* indicate that taking excursions to Jamestown Island, especially for picnics, was a popular local pastime and a special celebration was held there on May 13 nearly every year. None, however, rivaled the observance held in 1857.

❖

Portrait of William Allen. Courtesy of the Virginia Historical Society.

Chapter 9

❖

THE CLOUDS OF WAR

NORTH AGAINST SOUTH

The first shots fired at Fort Sumter, South Carolina, on April 12, 1861, signaled the beginning of the Civil War. Five days later, on April 17, Virginia voted to secede and, in May, Richmond became the Confederacy's capital. Before the end of the war the Union had launched a total of seven military campaigns to capture the Confederate capital.

Initially, small bodies of strategically placed troops defended the city's approaches. Confederate General Robert E. Lee also fortified the James River with water-batteries and earthworks, including five built on Jamestown Island. Collectively, these gun emplacements prevented Union naval vessels from circumventing Confederate land-based defenses built on the peninsula.

But the work of fortifying Richmond progressed so slowly that General Lee expressed his concern. Virginia's General Assembly responded by requiring all free black males between 18 and 50 to participate in public works projects, such as building fortifications. They had to register with their local court and could be called upon to serve up to 180 days at a time. Conscript workers received food, lodging, medical care, and compensation in exchange for the tasks they performed. Free blacks, slaves, and Confederate troops all helped construct the earthworks that took form on Jamestown Island and around Williamsburg.

JAMESTOWN ISLAND, A CONFEDERATE MILITARY BASE

William Allen occupied Jamestown Island immediately after Virginia seceded. He started to fortify it with troops he raised at his own expense, but Catesby ap Roger Jones, a naval lieutenant, arrived in May to construct gun batteries and assume command. "Owing to the course of the [river's] channel," which made it important strategically, the first battery was extensive, with five faces and provisions to install 18 guns. Jones was reinforced with infantry, and during the summer the Confederates' strength peaked at about 1,200 men, although this figure dwindled rapidly when units were transferred elsewhere.

The Confederate military engineer who was assigned to Jamestown later recalled that he had to build a bridge across the Back River for the army's use.

Armor found by Confederates. Courtesy of the National Park Service, Colonial National Historical Park.

He remembered seeing a mansion [the Ambler house] that was "not in very good repair but entirely habitable, and the ruins of the old church." There were "some small frame buildings at the shore end of the wharf." The island "was in a very good state of cultivation" and the engineer recollected General Lee's "bemoaning the sacrifice of a promising wheat field to a square redoubt." He added that "the battery, which was built just above the old tower, was not far from the brink of the river bank." A Confederate veteran's widow remembered her husband saying that "at low tide about 75 yards east of the old church" were "the brick walls of an old house, and from these walls his men obtained bricks for the fireplaces and chimneys of the tents."

In late May 1861, when Colonel (soon Major General) John B. Magruder assumed command of the forces between Jamestown Island and the York River, the Confederates erected a five-gun battery farther down the island. The steam tender, Teaser, ferried troops between the island and the mainland, as landings in the lower part of the James had become very risky. Magruder ordered Jamestown's commander to "keep a bright lookout" and, if necessary, to spike the batteries' guns and abandon the island. In July some of the cannon that did not bear directly upon the main channel were shifted to other locations. In September 1861, in anticipation of a Federal advance, troops received orders to abandon Jamestown Island if construction of bombproofs had not been finished.

In October the Confederates finished a series of ordnance and armor experiments on Jamestown Island that preceded final construction of their first ironclad vessel, the Virginia. Eight and nine-inch guns blasted 12-foot-square wooden targets positioned over 300 feet away and shielded with various types of iron in the final test.

By this time the Confederates had earthworks at five sites on Jamestown Island. The main one was near the old church tower, while one toward Back River guarded the bridge. A third was centrally located, and the others were at Black Point and Goose Hill. They also erected earthworks on the nearby main-

View from inside Fort Pocahontas. Courtesy of National Park Service, Colonial National Historical Park.

land. General Magruder considered Jamestown Island his army's right flank and the island's earthworks an integral part of Richmond's defenses.

ONSET OF THE PENINSULA CAMPAIGN

Early in 1862 Fort Monroe in Hampton became the Union Army's base of oper-ations for the Peninsula Campaign, an attempt to capture Richmond and bring the war to an early conclusion. But when Union Major General George B. McClellan arrived there, he had fewer troops than he had requested. Faced with what he considered a serious shortage of men and the need to commence his campaign, McClellan split his army into two columns to outflank the Confederates at Yorktown.

On April 4, 1862, McClellan and his men began their advance. One column paralleled the James River, turning inland at the Warwick Court House. Meanwhile, the other column marched toward Yorktown. General McClellan, cautious by nature, was hindered by inaccurate maps, adverse weather condi-tions, and inflated estimates of enemy strength.

Magruder's tactical skill and the strategic planning of General Joseph E. Johnston delayed the Union advance even further. Magruder initiated the process by erecting three parallel lines of earthworks across the peninsula, tak-ing maximum advantage of numerous creeks and ridges. His first line extended from Harwood's and Young's mills to the heads of the Poquoson and Warwick rivers, where the intervening solid ground consisted of a three-mile strip flanked by boggy and difficult swamps and streams. His second line ran from Yorktown to Mulberry Island, following the Warwick River, and his third, just outside of Williamsburg, included a string of earthworks that stretched between College and Queens creeks anchored by a large redoubt known as Fort Magruder. Jamestown Island was fortified with Dahlgrens, Columbiads, and Navy 32-pounders. Magruder, anticipating the Union Army advance, declared martial law throughout the region.

In mid-April General Johnston took command of the Confederate forces on the peninsula, and in May he ordered a retreat to the outskirts of Richmond. By this time his 65,000 men opposed an army of 95,000 men. As a result of Johnston's decision the Confederates abandoned their middle position (the Warwick line) and fell back toward Williamsburg, their westernmost and final line of defense.

THE BATTLE OF WILLIAMSBURG

On May 4, 1862, Union cavalry moved toward Williamsburg along the Yorktown Road and attacked Confederate infantry and cavalry east of King's Creek, but were repulsed. General Johnston, whose men had abandoned Yorktown the night before, ordered two brigades to occupy Fort Magruder, which they reached by nightfall amid cold, drenching rain. At daybreak on May 5 the Confederates held several redoubts that flanked Fort Magruder and controlled the roads to Yorktown and Hampton. Woods and thickets, too dense for artillery, lined the muddy roads.

When Union troops attacked the Confederate center and right, the Southerners employed a holding action that temporarily stopped the advance. Late in the afternoon the Union army gained the upper hand on the Confederate left. While both sides claimed victory, the Confederates' resistance checked McClellan for the night, enabling them to withdraw under cover of darkness. Only when the Union cavalry entered Williamsburg on the morning of May 6 did General McClellan learn that the Confederates had departed. The rear of the retreating Confederate column narrowly had slipped his grasp. Never prone to accept blame, McClellan sent word to his wife that "the battle of Williamsburg has proved a brilliant victory," adding that the town itself was "a beautiful little town and quite old and picturesque."

UNION OCCUPATION OF JAMESTOWN ISLAND

On May 20, 1862, Miss Harriette Cary, a Williamsburg resident, heard that "two Yankee gun boats [were] very much disabled by our batteries on the narrows of James River" [Drewry's Bluff] near Richmond. There were "many killed - 15 buried at James Town who had died of their wounds on their return." Initial

Confederate success, however, only slowed the Union advance. After the Union Army gained control of Williamsburg, they occupied Jamestown Island as well, maintaining a telegraph station there. In June the crew of the U. S. gunboat, Aroostook, burned the buildings, magazines, and carriages associated with Jamestown's Confederate gun batteries. They spiked all of the guns not disabled already. The only military structure spared was a barracks in the rear of the large battery on the western end of the island, then occupied by African Americans escaping from slavery. One naval officer recommended posting a guard on constant surveillance at Jamestown Island to prevent the Confederates from infiltrating what had become Union-held territory, but Jamestown was abandoned later that summer.

The USS Aroostock. Courtesy of the United States Naval Historical Center.

An event that occurred soon thereafter illustrates the civil unrest that often accompanied military campaigns. In October 1862 an estimated 100 African Americans from William Allen's Jamestown Island and Neck O'Land plantations shot and killed his main overseer, a child, and a relative of Allen's wife who visited the island. They burned Allen's buildings on the island and at his Neck O'Land and Kingsmill farms. The lone survivor was a free black employee of Allen's. Wounded and left for dead, he made his way to Surry County where he reported the incident. Union military authorities made little (if any) attempt to punish the perpetrators, although newspapers in Petersburg, Richmond, and Lynchburg demanded justice for what they described as cold-blooded, "fiendish murders."

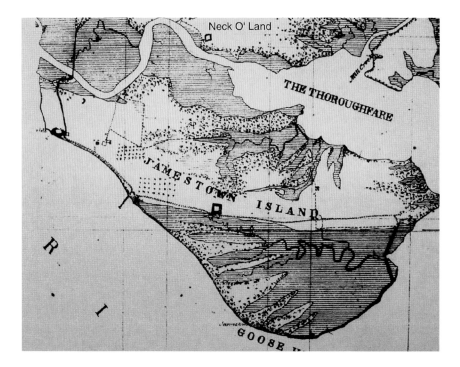

Detail from *James River from College Creek to the Chickahominy River, 1873-1874*. Topographic map by John W. Donn. Courtesy of the National Archives.

In the summer of 1863 Jamestown became an outpost for Union troops at Williamsburg, and the telegraph station was reactivated the following year. Companies of cavalry, infantry, artillery, and U.S. Colored Troops served in rotation to monitor Confederate guerillas and activity on the river. Although the men sometimes climbed to the top of the crumbling church tower to gain a better view, Captain David E. Cronin noted that the tower stood only a little higher than the nearby Confederate fortification. Union sentries were especially vigilant at night, when spies and smugglers attempted to cross the James. Each evening, to prevent the pickets from being overtaken from the rear, they removed a few boards from the plank bridge that connected Jamestown Island with the mainland.

Assuming prudent military alertness, the Federals considered Jamestown a good duty station. They had an abundance of fish, shellfish, and game, along with fruits and nuts. There was plenty of time for reading and the encampments near Williamsburg "did not lack for books of an entertaining kind, either light or serious, taken from the fine libraries found in the abandoned town mansions."

Nonetheless, life on the peninsula was dangerous as illustrated by other routine duties. On September 3, 1864, three members of the 20th New York

Cavalry escorted a Union ambulance, sent to Jamestown Island to retrieve three sick men. As they approached their destination, they were ambushed by Confederates concealed in the woods. Lieutenant John D. Lee, who led a party of Union cavalrymen on a retaliatory mission, concluded that the "guerilla party in question was composed of citizens of the neighborhood."

After General Lee surrendered to Lieutenant General Ulysses S. Grant on April 9, 1865, Jamestown served its final role in the war as a site where the Oath of Allegiance was administered to former Confederates.

The eroding river bank at Jamestown. *The Century Magazine* January-February 1891.
Courtesy of the National Park Service, Colonial National Historical Park.

MOVING AHEAD

THE AFTERMATH OF WAR

Virginia endured the full fury of the Civil War. Over 200 military engagements occurred within the state. Many of the state's towns and cities lay in shambles or had deteriorated through neglect. Throughout the rural countryside, fields were ruined, crops and livestock were gone, bridges and railroads were destroyed, and countless homes and businesses were irreparably damaged. An estimated 20,000 to 30,000 Virginia soldiers lost their lives and many thousands of others were permanently maimed as a result of war wounds and disease. Confederate money and bonds were worthless, inflation was at an all time high, and legal tender was almost nonexistent. Real estate values plummeted and land worth $50 an acre before the war afterward sold for $2. Virginia's industries sustained so much damage that the state failed to attain prewar production levels by 1870. For the first six months after the surrender at Appomattox, at least 25,000 white Virginians subsisted on army rations. The 13th Amendment to the U. S. Constitution ended slavery and forever altered the South's pre-war social order, but many of the 360,000 freed blacks lacked food, clothing, shelter, and the means to make a living.

Undoubtedly, numerous returning soldiers, already weary, malnourished, and saddened by the loss of comrades, were completely demoralized by the conditions they found at home. Neglected farmland had quickly sprouted dense vegetation. Young pines needed to be cleared before plowing. Predatory animals multiplied in the underbrush creating problems for those fortunate enough to own poultry and livestock.

Census records reveal that a considerable number of households consisted of unrelated individuals who apparently banded together for mutual support. Sharecroppers or leaseholders operated many farms. Sometimes, the freed slaves chose to stay on or near the plantations of their former owners. Throughout eastern Virginia, numerous rural landowners subdivided their farms or relinquished them altogether. Northern speculators with expendable capital sometimes purchased cheap land, often for back taxes. Court records demonstrate that while some Northern buyers relocated to the land they purchased, others quickly resold or subdivided farms hoping for a quick profit.

BLACK REFUGEES

At the close of the war, the James-York peninsula had a substantial population of free but homeless blacks. This influx of refugees, who often came with little more than the clothes on their backs and a few personal belongings, posed serious health and welfare problems for Federal authorities, both during and after the war. In 1865, to provide food, shelter, clothing, and fuel to "suffering refugees and freedmen and their wives and children," Congress established the Bureau of Refugees, Freedmen and Abandoned Lands. Bureau agents negotiated labor contracts for ex-slaves and arranged medical care and schooling, often in cooperation with the American Missionary Association and other private agencies. Armed with the authority to reallocate private property abandoned by owners or confiscated for back taxes, the bureau was vulnerable to accusations of seizing property punitively. In fact, because whites had left in droves when the Union Army swept up the peninsula, a substantial amount of vacant land was available. Typically, larger farms were subdivided into small parcels that refugees leased, paying rent in crop-shares. Among the local properties temporarily placed in the hands of free blacks were William Allen's Neck O'Land and Kingsmill farms; the confiscated property was restored to its owners of record in 1867.

THE PAIN OF RECOVERY

Local court records bear mute testimony to the hardships of Reconstruction. Thanks to the loss of farm income, some landowners were unable to pay for property purchased before the war. Many others became indebted to merchants and businesses. Local farmers faced labor shortages and worn out agricultural equipment. They lacked the funds they needed to buy seed, fertilizer, and livestock. Ultimately, a significant number forfeited their real and personal property or declared bankruptcy. The destruction of almost all of James City County's antebellum court records made it difficult for those buying and selling land to substantiate ownership claims.

JAMESTOWN ISLAND AFTER THE WAR

Ownership of Jamestown Island changed over and over again. Initially, in May 1865, William Allen of Claremont leased Jamestown Island to three New Yorkers and gave them authority to repair the farm's buildings and erect new ones. In 1868, before this lease expired, Allen sold the island to lessee George B. Field and another Northerner, Israel Williams. Williams moved to Jamestown Island, which he operated as a working farm. In 1871 he conveyed his interest in the island to Field, including "the dwellings, paper mill and other improvements" on the property. Soon Field, like Williams, fell upon hard times. In January 1874 he leased the island to Franklin Rowley and later sold it to Frederick Rollin of Brooklyn, New York.

JAMESTOWN AS A HISTORIC ATTRACTION

Although it continued to be difficult to keep track of the island's owners, Jamestown's history became the focus of increased attention. On May 15, 1877, Frederick Rollin's wife, Mamie, wrote a friend that there had been "quite a jubilee on the island yesterday," attended by a large number of visitors. She said that boats from Norfolk and Richmond made daily excursions to Jamestown and would do so throughout the summer. But the Rollins, like George Field, also fell prey to financial difficulties and defaulted on their mortgage.

As a result, in 1879, Francis and Lucy Clay Brown of Hampton bought Jamestown Island at a public auction. On May 13, 1889, faculty, students, and

The Jamestown Seawall about 1901. Courtesy of the National Park Service, Colonial National Historical Park.

alumni from the College of William and Mary staged a small celebration to commemorate the first settlers' arrival. In November 1892 the Browns sold Jamestown Island to Edward E. Barney and his wife, Louise, of Dayton, Ohio. The Barneys took up residence across the river and hired a man to oversee farming on Jamestown Island.

The approach of Jamestown's 300th anniversary generated a considerable amount of excitement. The 1807, 1822, and 1857 celebrations had demonstrated that there was a great deal of public interest in commemorating the first colonists' landing. By the early 1890s preparations were underway for the May 13, 1907, celebration. On March 1, 1892, nine months before the Barneys purchased Jamestown Island, the General Assembly conveyed the state's interest in the church ruins, cemetery, and churchyard to the Association for the Preservation of Virginia Antiquities (APVA) along with the right to acquire a right-of-way to the property through condemnation. On May 13, 1893, the Barneys deeded 22 1/2 acres to the APVA. The Barneys and the APVA agreed to share the cost of constructing "a wall or some other permanent means of preventing the further washing and caving of the bank" at the western end of Jamestown Island. The U. S. government provided $40,000 for the project, which was administered by the APVA.

One local resident, who witnessed construction of the concrete seawall, said that most of the men who built it earned $1.25 to $1.50 a day, whereas those who pushed the wheelbarrows containing bags of cement received an extra 25 cents. The majority of these laborers were African Americans, who reported to work each morning at 7 A.M. and typically put in a 10-hour day shoveling cement. Colonel Samuel H. Yonge of the Army Corps of Engineers, who oversaw construction, was a skillful engineer and a diligent scholar whose antiquarian interests led him to study the island's history and explore its archaeological features. His publication of *The Site of Old "James Towne"* in 1904 provided many insights into the history of America's first permanent English settlement.

Articles that appeared in the *Virginia Gazette* during 1893 reveal that Edward E. Barney, the young millionaire owner of Jamestown Island, planned to turn it into a tourist mecca. He proposed building a large, modern hotel with "magnificent style" that would "bring to that famous spot myriads of tourists and pleasure seekers." He also hoped to construct an electric railway linking Jamestown with Williamsburg and a bridge and causeway from Jamestown Island to the mainland. By providing new access to Jamestown, Barney intended to give "people an opportunity to visit and see the advantages of our country." But Barney's farm manager, George Bedell, told the press that his employer sought local investors for his projects and would await "a ground-swell of interest" before undertaking construction. Barney, meanwhile, erected "a splendid wharf" that extended into the James and held a large warehouse, storeroom, and pavilion.

Between June 1893 and June 1894 an estimated 5,000 tourists visited

Jamestown Island, despite the "deplorable condition" of the roads between there and Williamsburg. In May 1894 George Bedell informed the *Virginia Gazette* that the Barneys' employees were busily clearing underbrush, reclaiming marshland, and developing Jamestown Island into a truck farm and place of scenic interest. They installed a new artesian well, and the construction of a new causeway was underway. Excavators hired by the Barneys dug around the ancient ruins along the waterfront and near the church, recovering relics that Mrs. Barney prized. They unearthed what they termed brick subterranean passages or tunnels which they theorized had allowed the early settlers to escape from the Indians. They planned to put "an old fort...under glass." Farm manager Bedell recommended that the APVA (or "Antiquarian Society" as he called it) sell bricks at the Chicago World's Fair to offset the cost of readying the church site for tourists. Throughout 1893 and 1894 Jamestown Island bustled with activity.

The palace steamer, *Pocahontas*, made regular stops at Jamestown Island while Edward Barney was the Virginia Navigation Company's president. The Pocahontas, reportedly 205 feet long and 57 feet wide with a 2,100 horsepower engine, boasted every imaginable luxury, including "electric orchestrion giving full musical effects of a full band." Guests were invited to partake of water from Jamestown's artesian wells and fresh fruit and vegetables grown on the island.

In 1784 the Virginia legislature decided to give almost all publicly owned land, except church property, to the College of William and Mary and authorized college officials to sell it. In 1799 the General Assembly decided to dispose of all real estate formerly owned by the State church, except churches still in use. Nearly a century later, the 1799 law was resurrected when the legislature conveyed the ruinous James City Parish church and its abandoned graveyard to the Association for the Preservation of Virginia Antiquities.

In February 1895 ice on the James River destroyed part of the Barneys' new Jamestown Island wharf and on March 31 a blaze destroyed the Ambler house which had been renovated recently, leaving blackened and fire-cracked walls to tower over the landscape. Valuable personal belongings and $4,000 worth of furniture vanished in the fire. Unfortunate though it was, the destruction of the Barneys' house did not prevent the College of William and Mary and the APVA from jointly hosting a May 13, 1895, gala reportedly attended by 2,000 people.

Early in 1896 Barney signed over to his wife his legal interest in their Virginia properties and on August 1, 1896, he committed suicide. Mrs. Louise Barney continued to take an active interest in the Jamestown Island farm. In August 1906 she gave the Williamsburg and Jamestown Turnpike Company access to her wharf and a right-of-way to the APVA property in preparation for the 1907 tercentennial celebration.

Ambler House before the 1895 fire. Courtesy of the Naitonal Park Service, Colonial National Historical Park.

The West Virginia House, built at Seawell's Point for the 1907 Jamestown Exposition. Photograph, courtesy of Nan Maxwell.

The year 1907 was widely anticipated throughout Virginia. A variety of projects proceeded along parallel tracks, but all refocused attention on the colonial history of the island.

In 1900 Lyon G. Tyler published his first edition of *Cradle of the Republic*, in which he provided an overview of Jamestown Island's history. The discovery of revealing Ambler family manuscripts led him to make extensive revisions to his text, re-published under the same title in 1906.

In 1901 the General Assembly incorporated the Order of Jamestown 1607 with the express purpose of stimulating interest in the origins of the Episcopal Church in America. The new organization formulated plans to erect a monument to the Reverend Robert Hunt of Jamestown and to restore Bruton Parish Church, which had inherited the Jamestown Church's baptismal font and communion silver.

Two years later the Jamestown Exposition Company received a $200,000 appropriation from the General Assembly to develop a site at Norfolk's Sewell's Point for the 1907 celebration. As preparations moved forward, the General Assembly appropriated additional funds for the construction of buildings and displays. Special legislation permitted "soldiers and sailors of the United States and all foreign governments and all state militias to bear arms and maneuver at the Jamestown Exposition" and all of the guards at the exposition were appointed "conservators of the peace." The Virginia Historical Society began to prepare an exhibit of important documents for display during the exposition while Virginia counties prepared exhibits highlighting their industrial, agricultural, mineral, and commercial resources. Five-year-old Powhatan Durham, "mascot" of the Jamestown Exposition and the son of the APVA's first custodian at Jamestown, appeared at the exposition dressed in Indian garb. Young Durham reportedly had been born "in the old Confederate Fort . . . while his parents lived in a house that once stood within those ruined embankments."

The exposition operated from April 26 to November 30. President Theodore Roosevelt delivered the opening day address, and the Fourth Division of the U.S. Atlantic Fleet launched its voyage around the world with a display of American naval power during closing ceremonies.

After the Jamestown Exposition, the state conveyed the old tercentennial grounds to the United States government and the site became the Norfolk Naval Base. Some of the buildings constructed for the 1907 celebration still exist.

Virginians celebrated the tercentennial on the island as well. By 1906 plans were under way to erect a granite obelisk patterned after the Washington Monument on .126 acres of land near Jamestown's old church tower. The Daughters of the American Revolution undertook construction of a colonial-style building at Jamestown, and the APVA and descendants of Pocahontas independently commissioned sculptors to produce bronze statues of Captain John Smith and Pocahontas. The National Society, Colonial Dames of

America, hired experts to reconstruct the Jamestown Church while carefully preserving its original foundation.

CONTINUED INTEREST

With or without special anniversaries, Jamestown continued to attract local residents and tourists alike. Groups of picnickers and sightseers visited the island and enjoyed strolling around the ruins or walking along the riverbank. Cognizant of this continued interest, in February 1900 several local men formed

Jamestown Island, depicted in *Afloat on the James*, published in 1903 by the Virginia Navigation Company.

the Jamestown, Williamsburg, and Yorktown Railroad Company and received a charter from the state that allowed company officers to issue stock and to purchase or condemn land for a railroad between Jamestown and Yorktown. Charter provisions stipulated that the J, W, & Y had to start construction within two years and complete its work in five. It never happened and, in April 1902, the J, W, & Y consolidated with the Jamestown, Poquoson and Hampton Railroad to form the Jamestown and Old Point Comfort Railroad Company. Shortly thereafter, the new company received the James City County Board of Supervisors' permission to cross the county's public roads with its equipment. In the 19-teens, regular jitney service ran between Jamestown Island and Williamsburg on Sundays. During Prohibition, two Portsmouth men accidentally introduced air travel to Jamestown when their small plane made a forced landing on the island. When rescuers discovered that they were transporting liquor, both men ended up in jail.

In 1918 the General Assembly began planning for the 300th anniversary of America's first legislative assembly which had met in 1619. In the continuing battle between land and river, the bridge and causeway connecting Jamestown Island with the mainland were unusable again. Because the APVA lacked the funds needed for reconstruction, the Assembly passed a special appropriation to underwrite the cost.

Jamestown Island's popularity with tourists continued to grow. In October 1923 Mrs. Louise Barney leased Jamestown Island and its improvements to B. E. Steel for ten years. Steel made a subsidiary agreement with A. F. Jester, who intended to convert Mrs. Barney's wharf into a ferry landing and operate a boat to Surry County. Three years later a bill introduced in the United States Senate recommended that the federal government purchase Jamestown Island, but that legislation was tabled. In 1929 the state and federal governments did collaborate in the construction of a wharf and pier and the APVA made plans for excursion boats to land there. A steamship company which stopped at Jamestown even drilled an artesian well to accommodate thirsty visitors.

❖

C.C.C. workers washing artifacts in the Jamestown laboratory in 1938. Courtesy of the National Park Service, Colonial National Historical Park.

REVERENCE FOR THE PAST,
A VIEW TOWARD THE FUTURE

Jamestown's past remained a source of curiosity as first one group and then another rediscovered the island's history. In 1928 Chesapeake and Ohio Railroad agricultural agent, C. J. Jehne, purchased 5 1/2 acres at Glasshouse Point, the site of glassmaking operations during the first quarter of the seventeenth century. Jesse Dimmick, then-owner of the Main farm or Amblers-On-The-James, discovered portions of four furnaces in which glass had been manufactured. Mr. Jehne donated his land at Glasshouse Point to the James City County 4-H program, whose club members used it until the 1940s, when it was acquired by the National Park Service (NPS). During the first few months of 1931, students from the Riordon Boys School of Highland, New York, attended classes at Jamestown aboard the steamship, Southland, anchored at the new "government dock." As a goodwill gesture to their host community, the boys planted a thousand trees sent to Virginia by the New York Conservation Commission. And in 1936 black evangelist Elder Lightfoot Solomon Michaux and his followers purchased a 1,000-acre farm near Jamestown Island hoping to establish a school for delinquent children and a museum commemorating the arrival of Virginia's first blacks. When a lack of funding curtailed construction, the property became known as the Gospel Spreading Farm. Special prayer services were held at the farm on holidays and other occasions. The National Memorial Park, an amusement area with a small museum honoring Elder Michaux, overlooked the river until the property became part of the Colonial Parkway's right-of-way.

In 1947 the Jamestown Corporation, a non-profit educational group, built an amphitheater at Lake Matoaka in Williamsburg and began staging an outdoor drama, the *Common Glory*, about the American Revolution. The play, supported by the College of William and Mary and the Commonwealth of Virginia, was performed nightly every summer through 1976, becoming a favorite with locals and tourists. In 1957, as part of Jamestown's 350th anniversary, a second historical drama, *The Founders*, was added to the theater company's repertoire. This drama focused on Jamestown's earliest years. It closed after two years, was revived in 1964, and closed again.

CREATION OF COLONIAL NATIONAL MONUMENT

In January 1930 Congressman Louis C. Crampton introduced a bill into the House of Representatives giving the Secretary of the Interior the authority to designate historic sites in Jamestown, Yorktown, and part of Williamsburg as Colonial National Monument. Crampton envisioned a scenic boulevard linking the individual sites. Local citizens hotly debated the Crampton bill; many viewed it as a major intrusion of "big government." In early February 1930 the James City County Board of Supervisors made their opposition part of the public record. Congressman Crampton attempted to reassure local officials that his bill was intended to foster cooperation and, in June, Secretary of the Interior, Ray Lyman Wilbur, made a personal visit to the area to promote Crampton's idea. In 1930 an act of Congress coupled with a presidential proclamation heralded official creation of Colonial National Monument.

Planning began immediately, beginning with a breakwater around Jamestown Island. Marshes were to be drained and shrubs and trees planted to retard erosion. Some talked about restoring historic buildings. During the late summer an army dirigible began taking aerial photographs of Williamsburg and Jamestown on behalf of the Colonial National Monument Commission. In August the state joined the effort by authorizing a private group of investors to raise funds to build a bridge from Surry County to the island. The project languished for lack of public support. Meanwhile, tourists continued to visit the island; an estimated 36,000 tourists arrived in 1931. The improvement of roads in Surry County led to increased visitation and a Jamestown ferry captain offered a color picture of Captain John Smith to the driver of every passenger vehicle he took across the river on Sunday, February 28. Steamships docked regularly at Jamestown, some from as far away as Baltimore. Every spring there were small commemorative events.

The government planned to purchase all of Jamestown Island except that portion owned by the APVA. Mrs. Barney's stubborn refusal to sell her land led to a bitterly contested lawsuit. When the Department of the Interior finally acquired the bulk of Jamestown Island in 1934, it turned to the National Park Service for on-site management. Surveyors laid out the parkway that the Crampton bill thought should link Jamestown to Williamsburg and Yorktown. Administratively, Colonial National Monument's name changed to Colonial National Historical Park in 1936. In December 1940 Congress recognized the special relationship that existed between the APVA and the U. S. government.

Via a cooperative agreement both groups agreed to provide a uniform program of development and to jointly administer the island.

THE CCC AND JAMESTOWN ISLAND

During the Great Depression, as unemployment spiraled upward, President Franklin D. Roosevelt initiated the Emergency Conservation Work Program, or Civilian Conservation Corps (CCC). The CCC linked employment to conservation. Designed for single males between the ages of 18 and 25 whose families were receiving welfare, each CCC enrollee earned a dollar a day, $25 of which was sent home to his family. CCC enrollees, chosen by city and county welfare officials and the U. S. Employment Service, were processed by the Army Recruiting Service, which gave them a physical examination and issued them World War I surplus clothing. Military personnel commanded each 200-man CCC company.

In July 1933 William and Mary administrators requested CCC workers to develop part of the college's woods and lake into a park. The tents of Camp Matoaka (or Camp SP-9) began to appear on the William and Mary campus in the fall and, before Thanksgiving, the CCC had replaced the tents with frame buildings. Sixteen local white men supervised the workers, who were black. First, the CCC repaired damage from a 1932 hurricane. Next, they constructed roads, trails, picnic areas, and a large outdoor amphitheater in the college woods.

Soon they began work on Jamestown Island. Erosion control projects followed initial island clean-up; one of the CCC's most important contributions on Jamestown Island was construction of rip-rap. For four years, workers arrived daily from the college campus with a few serving as night and weekend watchmen. Some CCC units assigned to Colonel J. P. Barney, whose parents once owned Jamestown Island, conducted archaeological excavations under the supervision of the NPS.

During 1940 and 1941 the CCC worked along the Colonial Parkway, planting trees and grass from Yorktown to Williamsburg and placing fill over the newly completed tunnel beneath Williamsburg's historic area. On April 15, 1942, Williamsburg's CCC camp was closed. The United States had entered World War II and Congress denied President Roosevelt's request for CCC funding.

During the latter part of World War II the Colonial Parkway tunnel was designated an air raid shelter. But it was not until 1949 that the tunnel opened to automobile traffic, and it was not until 1957 that the section between Williamsburg and Jamestown was completed.

JAMESTOWN'S 350TH BIRTHDAY

The early 1950s brought a resurgence of interest in Jamestown, with the approach of the 350th anniversary of the first colonists' arrival. The Glass Crafters of America offered $1,000 toward moving Pocahontas's remains from an

Queen Elizabeth II and Prince Phillip of England attend the Jamestown Festival. Courtesy of the Jamestown-Yorktown Foundation.

unmarked grave in a church cemetery in Gravesend, England, to Virginia. The proposal failed when the church rector expressed his opposition to disinterring Pocahontas, if indeed her grave could be identified.

But an elaborate celebration in 1957 called the Jamestown Festival did attract large crowds, including Queen Elizabeth II and Prince Philip of England, and Vice President Richard M. Nixon. The NPS conducted extensive archaeological excavations on both NPS and APVA properties, the NPS erected a visitor center, and a state facility known as Jamestown Festival Park (later renamed Jamestown Settlement) opened to the public. Virginia artist Sidney E. King produced a series of paintings that recreated Jamestown streetscapes. Historical booklets offered visitors ample background reading. The Colonial Parkway finally linked Williamsburg to Jamestown and a causeway connected Jamestown Island with the mainland. To commemorate the arrival of Virginia's first Africans, a special ceremony was held at the Jamestown Festival Park where black military officers were honored and a salute was fired in recognition of World War II naval hero Dorie Miller. In 1960 Native Americans from several states began holding an annual Fall Festival at Jamestown Festival Park.

ARCHAEOLOGY AT JAMESTOWN

As interest in Jamestown grew, relic hunters searched for artifacts that lay beneath the soil. During the 1890s, when the Barneys owned Jamestown Island, workmen excavated some of the old brick foundations in the New Towne area. In 1897 APVA founder, Mary Jeffery Galt, supervised excavations at the site of the old church tower and attempted to mark the graveyard. Members examined a number of graves, retrieved artifacts that caught their attention, and tried to decipher and preserve whatever burial markers they found. They also sought the advice of Lyon G. Tyler, president of the College of William and Mary, who, in June 1901, prepared a written report of his excavations at the church site. Colonel Samuel H. Yonge of the Corps of Engineers, who built Jamestown Island's seawall, found the rowhouse known as the Ludwell Statehouse Group and conducted excavations there in 1903. During the late 1920s a Richmond banker and antiquarian, George C. Gregory, interpreted archaeological features at Jamestown.

After the United States government acquired Mrs. Barney's land on Jamestown Island, archaeological excavations were undertaken by the CCC. Between 1934 and 1936, John T. Zaharov, H. Summerfield Day, Alonzo W. Pond, and W. J. Winter excavated cultural features, portions of the New Towne, and adjacent areas. Architectural historian Henry Chandlee Foreman forbade the

Jamestown Archeological Assessment

The National Park Service conducted major archeological studies in the 1930s and 1950s. In 1992, a new project was launched, the Jamestown Archeological Assessment (JAA). This five-year program represented a partnership between the National Park Service, the Colonial Williamsburg Foundation, and the College of William and Mary.

The JAA combined many disciplines in an attempt to learn more about the diverse and compelling stories of Jamestown. Here are some of the results:

- archeologists surveyed the entire island, revealing nearly sixty formerly unknown archeological sites.

- scientists tested new data-collecting techniques and determined which would be the most effective for future excavations.

- archeologists uncovered American Indian settlements dating back over 10,000 years.

- pollen analysis revealed flora found on the island at the time of settlement.

- examination of tree rings revealed major droughts during crucial settlement years.

- intensive study of primary accounts allowed historians to create biographical listings of people associated with Jamestown and the property they owned.

archaeologists from excavating any closer than three feet from brick foundations. He felt that only specialists had the qualifications to examine colonial construction. In time, a considerable amount of antagonism developed between Foreman and the trained archaeologists. Nonetheless, field crews recovered, cleaned, and cataloged an abundance of artifacts.

In the fall of 1936 a new team of excavators, headed by J. C. Harrington, arrived at Jamestown. An archaeologist with experience in recording historic structures, he advocated the public interpretation of archaeology and expanded the archaeological program until it was interrupted by World War II. In the post war years Harrington conducted excavations at Glasshouse Point, where he unearthed the remains of four stone furnaces and several other features associated with Jamestown's glasshouse.

From 1954 to 1956 another NPS archaeological team, headed by John L. Cotter, conducted excavations at Jamestown and at the site of Governor William Berkeley's manor at Green Spring. This project emphasized the discovery of new buildings and features that would aid in park interpretation. Archaeologists carefully noted the context of each recovered artifact. Archaeological sites were marked with signs, and Sidney King paintings provided a visual interpretation of Jamestown's appearance.

Jamestown Rediscovery

Previous archeological work had failed to find evidence of the remains of James Fort. The Jamestown Rediscovery excavations, sponsored by the Association for the Preservation of Virginia Antiquities, began April 4, 1994. By 1996, archeologists had determined that the remains of the fort had not eroded into the James River, as many had conjectured.

As of 2000, seven seasons of excavation uncovered over 350,000 artifacts dating to the first half of the seventeenth century. Archeologists have excavated over 200 feet of the 1607 fort's palisade line, the east bulwark, two large trash pits, a post-in-ground structure and a large cellar, possibly part of a blockhouse.

More recently, in 1992, the NPS undertook a comprehensive archaeological assessment of the island. This on-going inter-disciplinary study, which utilizes the interdependency of natural and cultural factors as well as excavations, is being conducted by specialists from the NPS, the Colonial Williamsburg Foundation, and the College of William and Mary. On the western end of the island the APVA is sponsoring an ongoing archaeological study focusing on the remains of the fortifications that the first colonists built. Both studies are expected to shed new light on Jamestown Island's history in time for 2007, the 400th anniversary celebration.

❖

left: NPS Archeologists J. C. Harrington and Virginia Sutton (later Mrs. J., C. Harrington) addressing a group from William and Mary at Jamestown. Courtesy of the National Park Service, Colonial National Historical Park.

right: NPS Archeologist John L. Cotter with Pile Driver from the 1950s Jamestown excavations. Courtesy of the National Park Service, Colonial National Historical Park.

J. Paul Hudson, NPS, curator (on right), and Burley Green, lab assistant, sorting Jamestown artifacts from Project 103. Courtesy of the National Park Service, Colonial National Historical Park.

Scenic Jamestown Island Marshland.
Courtesy of the National Park Service,
Colonial National Historical Park.

Audrey Horning, Colonial Williamsburg Foundation Archaeologist, working on the
Jamestown Archeological Assessment Project in 1993. Courtesy of the Colonial
Williamsburg Foundation.

Aerial photo of Jamestown Island in 1997 by Air Survey Corporation. Courtesy of the National Park Service, Colonial National Historical Park.

EPILOGUE

The establishment of Jamestown on May 13, 1607, was a watershed event in the history of mankind. It left lasting legacies. For the native people whose ancestors inhabited the eastern portion of the American continent literally thousands of years before the arrival of the English adventurers, there was abrupt and irrevocable change.

The Europeans, who arrived first in small numbers and then by the thousands, sought opportunities that were out of reach in their ancestral homelands. Yet all would not succeed, and many suffered untimely deaths. Africans, who were torn from their families and transported thousands of miles from home, undoubtedly longed to gain their freedom. In time, their descendants' labor would support the economic prosperity of certain colonies and sections of America. The Civil War set them free.

Yet the legacies of Jamestown transcend the pain and sacrifices of so many. Here, a form of representative government was established. It began with the July 30, 1619, meeting of America's first legislative assembly. In time, a bicameral legislature served the Virginia colonists. During the Constitutional Convention in 1787, the founding fathers perpetuated this form of government by establishing the United States Congress and its two legislative chambers, the Senate and House of Representatives.

The sacrifices of men, women, and children of many ethnic and social backgrounds are exemplified in the story of Jamestown, from prehistoric times to the recent past. Adaptation and success are noble legacies that engender pride. Yet other aspects of the Jamestown story, such as the rise of slavery and the mistreatment of Virginia Indians, represent the worst of the American past and must not be forgotten. But perhaps Jamestown's most important legacy is what resulted from the mixing and adaptation of the cultures and peoples from diverse backgrounds. It symbolizes one of America's greatest achievements —the ability to draw strength from diversity.

The 104 settlers, who arrived in 1607on the Susan Constant, the Discovery, and the Godspeed, envisioned their new home as a land of vast opportunity, a place for the fulfillment of their dreams. Today, thousands immigrate to the United States of America, holding tightly to the same aspirations. For all of these reasons, Jamestown is commemorated and preserved as an American legacy.

The Jamestown Tercentary Monument erected by the Federal Government in 1907 to commemorate the 300th anniversary of the founding of Jamestown. Courtesy of the National Park Service, Colonial National Historical Park.

SELECTED SOURCES

AMBLER MANUSCRIPTS

1636-1809 Library of Congress, Washington, D. C. Transcripts and
microfilm, Rockefeller Library, Colonial Williamsburg
Foundation, Williamsburg.

BARBOUR, PHILIP L.

1969 *The Jamestown Voyages Under the First Charter, 1606- 1609.*
2 vols. University Press, Cambridge.

COLONIAL OFFICE (C.O.)

1607-1747 Colonial Office Papers, British Public Records Office, Kew,
England. Survey Reports and Microfilms, Rockefeller Library,
Colonial Williamsburg Foundation, Williamsburg.

HAMOR, RALPH

1957 *A True Discourse of the Present Estate of Virginia and the
Successe of the Affaires There till the 18th of June 1614.*
Virginia State Library, Richmond.

HENING, WILLIAM W., ED.

1809-1823 *The Statutes At Large: Being a Collection of All the Laws of
Virginia.* 13 vols. Samuel Pleasants, Richmond. Reprinted
1967, 1969.

KINGSBURY, SUSAN M.

1906-1935 Records of the Virginia Company of London. 4 vols.
Government Printing Office, Washington.

KULIKOFF, ALLAN

1986 *Tobacco and Slaves: The Development of Southern Cultures
in the Chesapeake, 1680-1800.* University of North
Carolina Press, Chapel Hill.

RIGGS, DAVID F.

1997 *Embattled Shrine: Jamestown in the Civil War.* White Mane
Publishing Company, Shippensburg, Penna.

ROLFE, JOHN

1957 *A True Relation of the State of Virginia Lefte by Sir Thomas
Dale Knight in May Last 1616.* University Press of Virginia,
Charlottesville.

ROUNTREE, HELEN C.

1990   *Pocahontas' People: The Powhatan Indians of Virginia.*
University of Oklahoma Press, Norman, Oklahoma.

SMITH, JOHN

1986   *Travels and Works of Captain John Smith, President of Virginia
and Admiral of New England, 1580-1631.* Philip Barbour, ed.
3 vols. University of North Carolina, Chapel Hill.

TATE, THAD AND DAVID AMMERMAN, EDS.

1979   *The Chesapeake in the Seventeenth Century.* University of
North Carolina Press, Chapel Hill.

WASHBURN, WILCOMB E.

1972   *The Governor and the Rebel: A History of Bacon's Rebellion
in Virginia.* W. W. Norton, New York.

WINFREE, WAVERLEY K.

1971   *The Laws of Virginia Being a Supplement to Hening's The
Statutes at Large, 1700-1750.* Virginia State Library, Richmond.

View of New Towne Foundations along the James River. Courtesy of the National Park Service,
Colonial National Historical Park.